Robin Hood

Silvatici

Echoes from the past, and the probable, yet controversial truth behind the Legend....

By Paul Glover

Grosvenor House
Publishing Limited

All rights reserved
Copyright © Paul Glover, 2025

All rights reserved, including the right of reproduction,
in any form unless written permission is granted by the Publisher,
together with the Author.

The right of Paul Glover to be identified as the author of this
work has been asserted in accordance with Section 78
of the Copyright, Designs and Patents Act 1988

The book cover is copyright to Paul Glover
Cover images copyright to:
Artem Zatsepilin, courtesy of Adobe Stock. Generated using AI
David Matthew Lyons, courtesy of Adobe Stock

This book is published by
Grosvenor House Publishing Ltd
Link House
140 The Broadway, Tolworth, Surrey, KT6 7HT.
www.grosvenorhousepublishing.co.uk

This book is sold subject to the conditions that it shall not, by way of
trade or otherwise, be lent, resold, hired out or otherwise circulated
without the author's or publisher's prior consent in any form of
binding or cover other than that in which it is published and
without a similar condition including this condition being
imposed on the subsequent purchaser.

A CIP record for this book
is available from the British Library

Paperback ISBN 978-1-83615-125-8
Hardback ISBN 978-1-83615-126-5
eBook ISBN 978-1-83615-127-2

Morality Question

Before we start this adventure, would you class Robin Hood
as a criminal, given that he stole from the rich and gave to the poor?
Or do you think he was in fact a good fellow?

Above: The greenwood.

Acknowledgements

Yet again, it is my wife who is the driving force behind writing this book. Her solid faith in me has given me the repeated energy to write this second book. I will always cherish the encouragement that she has given me. Gemaima, I love and thank you greatly. To my daughter Ellie, we all go through challenges in our life, but I want her to know that I will always love her. To Ricky, my trusted friend, what a journey we have been on! He has shared the mind-blowing experiences and discussions we have had surrounding this subject, and others, and I could not have achieved this without his dedication and commitment. This truly is a magical world!

The author and Ricky standing next to some of the ancient stones of Avebury one summer night, with a full moon in the background.

In Sherwood Livde Stout Robin Hood

In Sherwood Livde Stout Robin Hood
An archer great, none greater;
His bow and shafts were sure and good,
Yet Cupid's were much better.
Robin could shoot at many a hart and misse,
Cupid at first could hit a hart of his,
Hey jolly Robin hoe jolly Robin, hey jolly Robin Hood.

Love finds out me, as well as thee, so follow me,
So follow me to the green-wood.

A noble theife was Robin Hoode,
Wise was he could deceive him;
Yet Marrian, in his bravest mood,
Could of his heart berieve him!
No gteater theif lies hidden under the skies
Then beauty closely lodge in womans eyes,
Hey jolly Robin etc…

An out-law was this Robin Hood,
His life free and unruly;
Yet to faire Marrian bound he stood,
And loves debt paid her duly.
Whom curbe the strictest law could not hold in,
Love with obeyedness and winke could winne.
Hey jolly Robin etc..

Now wend we home, stout Robin Hood,
Leave we the woods behind us;
Love-passions must not be withstood,
Love every where will find us,
I lived in fielde and downe, and so did he,
I got me to the woods, love follow'd me.
Hey jolly Robin etc..

This comes from a musical dream, or the fourth book of Ayres, composed by Robert Jones, London. Printed in 1606.

Preface

The history of England is truly fascinating. For such a small piece of land on the surface of the globe, this country, sitting within the British Isles, has given the world a lot to talk about. It's history is vast and complex, both from a geological standpoint and then all the way through to the modern age. The earliest of its human inhabitants can be traced back 500,000 years ago to one of our distant relatives – Homo heidelbergensis, from Boxgrove in Sussex (where their remains were found). Even earlier, 900,000 years ago there is evidence of earlier habitation with primitive stone tools and footprints being found at Happisburgh on the Norfolk coast, yet of an unknown homo ancestor. These are considered the oldest fossil Homo footprints found outside of Africa. You will appreciate then that history is like a huge jigsaw puzzle, where you only have a few pieces of the puzzle, and you are trying to work out what the overall picture is/was. Like with fossil human remains, the earlier you go back in time, then the more difficult it is to find evidence for them. Lack of evidence is not evidence of absence. And this is not restricted to archaeology. Historians suffer with the same issues due to the lack of information from the time periods that they are studying. This is very true of the subject that we are going to tackle within this book. A thousand years ago, following the dark ages – 5th to 10th centuries, English society was making progress in recording things, mostly still in Latin, yet far from what we would wish for today, as very few people could read and write at this time. By the way, they were called the 'dark ages' due to the lack of information that we have about this period, plus the presumed decline in society following the fall of the Roman Empire. That said, remarkable discoveries such as the Sutton Hoo finds teach us that England was also flourishing during this time period and the people were creating some exceptional and intricate pieces of metal artwork. For me, there are many stages of British history that appeals and the Sutton Hoo ship burial is certainly one of them. Yet England itself has gone through some very dark times, as well as some good periods, and yet if I was to ask any historian what the year in English history that was so significant and important to the country, then I am sure that the vast majority will answer 1066.

The Norman Invasion of 1066 rocked the country to its core. Since the days of Athelstan (Æthelstan) – who beat all the Vikings to become the first true King of a united England (between 927 and 939), through to 1066, England remained a relatively peaceful and prosperous Anglo-Saxon nation. It had its own laws, customs, traditions, language and above all leadership/hierarchy. It basically had its own identity. That peace was all about to change, and if history is to be believed, then that fate was sealed by the flight of a single arrow. A chance hit in the eye of the newly crowned King, Harold II. Until then, the battle of Hastings was hanging in the balance. Had Harold held his ground till nightfall, then the outcome for England would have been very different. We will just never know how different things could have been, but most likely there would never have been the Hundred Years War with France.

William might have conquered Harold that day, but had he won the war? Well, taking England was not a forgone conclusion and just like the battle of Hastings, its success hung in the balance for a few years before the country was considered at peace again. They say that history is written by the victors, but is that always true?

So, with that in mind, let us now depart upon an adventure to the period of the Norman influence on England!

Before we start, I just want to add that I am no academic in this field. I enjoy studying history and never in my wildest dreams would I have imagined that I would end up writing a book on this subject. That said, this is now my second book, and the first one is a true mind blower and will take the reader time to take things on board, as it basically turns people's minds upside down. It will be years before my findings are accepted. Likewise, I think it is fair to say that this book is a game changer too..... and my hope is that this book will follow in a similar way. In summary, we need to start looking at things very differently if we are going to find answers to this very great English Legend!

Above: Springtime in the forest. And a teaser.

Background

It is the 21st Century now, the values and principles that we place upon ourselves are very different to the way it was over 800 years ago. So, in order to 'attempt' to understand this, we need to appreciate the background to the environment that the tales of Robin Hood came from.

In 1066 William of Normandy (William the Conqueror – who was of Viking descent – great-great-great grandson of Viking Ruler Rollo) invaded Southern England and beat the Anglo-Saxon King Harold Godwinson in an all-day battle at Hastings on the 14th. of October. It was a close call, but William won the day, he won the battle, yet did this mean he had won the war to rule this new territory?

Above: A medieval arrowhead. Was it one just like this that sealed the fate of England in 1066?

William was now faced with English nobility that did not support him, risk of uprisings and, also threats from Vikings in the East. His answer to this was brutality. The Norman Conquest was a seismic shift in the established Anglo-Saxon culture. He started by dividing the country into shires (previously established by the Anglo-Saxons), which were then divided into hundreds (basically patches of land accommodating 100 dwellings/farms/holdings) and each shire would be administered by a Royal Official called a 'Reeve' or 'King's representative' so, 'Shire Reeve' which then became shortened to 'Sheriff'. Strict Feudal Law was imposed, stripping English nobles of powers and Saxon Earls became 'tenants-in-chief' accountable to the new King. Due to various uprisings, William started a campaign of building many castles around the country and in order to appease some nobility, marriages were arranged, lands given, and sweeteners made in order to gain loyalty to this new King. Relatives of former King Harold II and those that fought at Hastings (and any associated uprisings) were to lose all their lands and wealth. William was harsh on both the innocent and the guilty....

This was a complex time, as many revolts took place, and these were crushed by brutal means. The 'Harrying of the North' by William's army during 1069-70 was merciless slaughter and pillaging of Northumbria, which it is estimated, led to the deaths of over 100,000 people due to either being killed or due to later starvation. These were truly 'brutal' days for England. With William's new control sealed, in 1086 he commissioned the 'Winchester Book' or 'Great Survey', later called the 'Doomsday Book' by the people of this time. The Anglo-Saxon Chronicle confirmed in 1085 that the King sent his agents to survey every Shire in England to list people and holdings and any 'dues' owed to him. In total, 268,984 people are tallied in the survey (this figure would have related to the 'head' of a household, but not all homes were included, this also excluded landless men). It is estimated that the total population at this time was around 1.2 to 1.6 million people. Over 90% of the population were peasants/serfs/poor people who worked for, or were overseen, by the new Norman Barons. William was here to stay, and he only achieved this through his harsh measures.

This invasion was the staging ground for discontent throughout the lands. When William, Duke of Normandy, invaded England, the country had been a single Kingdom for 150 years under Anglo-Saxon rule, following King Alfred's (The Great) and Athelstan's victories over the Vikings. The population at this time was mainly Anglo-Saxons with scattered people of Viking decent (mainly in the North and East). Was William's claim to the English throne legitimate? Well, Scholars can argue over this, but we understand that in 1051, Edward the Confessor had promised him the throne (he was a distant cousin), and later in 1064, Harold had sworn to uphold William's right to succeed to the throne. However, on Edward's deathbed, he named Harold as his successor, despite promising the throne to William. So, Harold, not only had the dying wishes of Edward, but he also had the support of the 'Witan' (advisers to the King) and all the English nobility were also in agreement. Edward the Confessor died on the

5th of January, 1066. The scene was now set for a show-down, yet we already know how this all played out.

William, Duke of Normandy, also known as Guillaume de Normandie, William the Bastard, Guillaume le Batard, William the Conqueror, Guillaume le Conquerant.

William 'the Bastard' is probably best how the Saxon people knew him to be at the time, yet this was also correct in the sense that he was the illegitimate son of Duke Robert I of Normandy and the daughter of a tanner from Falaise. It is evident that he was aware that he was not welcome as the new rightful King of the land, so he ruled with an iron fist. This would have been a major upheaval to the established status quo. Saxon nobility was replaced with Norman Lords. New laws relative to political, economic and social changes were all introduced, paving the way for huge discontent for the native people.

Above: William 1st – the Conqueror, silver penny (Bonnet Type) minted in Oxford 1068 – 1070.

'England has become a residence for foreigners and the property of strangers. At the present time there is no English earl nor bishop nor abbot; foreigners all they prey upon the riches and vitals of England'.

William of Malmesbury, 1135.

Although at the start, William wanted to appeal to the nation and seek peace, even starting to learn some English, however he is better known as being a tyrant King following the rebellions of the North. What started off as appeasing the natives, soon turned into controlling them with an iron fist. In order to control this defeated nation, he introduced several new laws.

Some of these laws included:

- Feudal Law: The Crown now technically owned all lands and any lands given to people, then they had to pay monies/taxes to the king and provide men for military service.
- Only one God and one faith will be worshipped throughout the Kingdom
- All men who want to be classed as freeman will swear an oath that they will be loyal to the new King and will defend his realm. Note: After proclaiming himself King, William got the English men to surrender their weapons, however because the Saxon archers had posed little threat at Hastings, William allowed them to keep their bows (with some exceptions related to the Royal Forests). As a result, the bow quickly became the symbol of free Englishman and why this became such a dominant force in the future centuries.
- All Normans that ventured to England will receive the Kings protection. As a result, the Normans introduced a special law, the 'Murdum' fine, in the hope that it would prevent hostilities towards them, as you can imagine the local Anglo-Saxons had grudges to settle. This is where we get the term 'murder' from. If a Norman had been killed and the murderer had not been found and executed within 5 days, then the local community would have to pay a fine (up to 46 marks of silver). This was restricted to the local 'hundred' where the body had been found in. Naturally, with all the taxes imposed on them, this would be another deterrent to any uprising.
- Forest Laws. People in the Kings forests were not allowed bow and arrows, or dogs. Wild game was not to be taken. The cutting down of trees was also not allowed. Heavy penalties were given for those that did not adhere to these conditions.
- Inheritance Laws: Under Anglo-Saxon laws, property was divided amongst all sons, however the Normans changed this so that only the eldest son inherited property. This was known as Primogeniture. This helped the Normans keep their vast estates long term.
- No live cattle can be sold outside of a city, and there needed to be three witnesses to oversee any sales transactions.
- No man is allowed to make sale for another man, basically abolishing slavery within England. Breaking this law would incur a fine to the King.

There were others.... but this gives you a flavour as to how things changed in England under Norman rule.

So, what were the causes that made William decide to become more of a tyrant rather than a loving and accommodating King? Well, basically, the people were not ready to concede to this military takeover and that resistance started immediately.

The different rebellions during William's first few years

Above: A Norman archer as featured in the Bayeux tapestry.

1067 – The start of resistance

Eadric the Wild began the armed Anglo-Saxon resistance in the Welsh Marcher Lands. Together with his allies from Wales – Princes Bleddyn and Rhiwallon, they overran Hereford (bar capturing the castle), and then retreating back to Wales and running guerrilla operations against the Norman forces.

Eadric was later behind more intense resistance in 1069, with the sacking of Shrewsbury and surrounding area, culminating with the Battle of Stafford against King William himself, who had travelled from more significant uprisings in the North.

1068 Rebellion in the North

Northumbria became a problem for William. The Earl of Northumbria, Morcar, had been replaced by William in 1066, however the following two earls were murdered (Copsi and Osulf). Cospatrick, a high-ranking Anglo-Saxon paid William to become the next Earl. Having been accepted, he soon changed his mind by siding with a rebellion led by Edwin of Mercia and later, Edgar Atheling. Support for this rebellion grew given that William decided to install Robert de Commines (a Norman) as the new Earl of Northumbria. Robert's arrival at Durham on the 28th of January, 1069, together with his army of 900 men, were all massacred. Eadgar, (Grandson of Edmund Ironside) the last Wessex claimant to the English throne, only joined the Rebellion following the sacking of Durham. Following Durham, the Rebellion moved on to York – where the guardian of the Castle, together with a large number of men, were all killed.

1069–1070 – Harrying of the North

Following the sacking of Durham and attacking of York, William rode North with a formidable force ready for combat and then swiftly retaking York. However, the main force of the Northern rebellion did not want to meet William on open ground and dispersed into the local countryside. William spent Christmas at York in 1069.

It was during the winter of 1069/70 that William will be remembered for just how brutal he was against the people of the North in his attempts to keep control of his Kingdom. The term 'Harrying of the North' have been described by some scholars as an act of genocide and a stain upon William's legacy. Ordric Vitalis (an Anglo- Norman Chronicler) wrote:

> *'he made no effort to restrain his fury and punished the innocent with the guilty. In his anger he commanded that all crops, herds and food of any kind be brought together and burned to ashes so that the whole region north of the Humber be deprived of any source of sustenance'.*

A later account written in the 12th century by Symeon of Durham (An English chronicler and a Monk from Durham) wrote:

> '... so great a famine prevailed that men, compelled by hunger, devoured human flesh, that of horses, dogs, and cats, and whatever custom abhors; others sold themselves to perpetual slavery, so that they might in any way preserve their wretched existence.'

The rebellion fizzled away, with many fleeing to Scotland or other parts of the country, yet many more dying of famine, illness or due to cruel Norman oppression. Due to the Rebellions in the North, there were several uprisings in Dorset, Devon and parts of the Midlands. William sent some of his Earls to deal with these, while he himself focused upon the new uprising by Eadric and the Welsh Princes. This ended with the Battle of Stafford.

1070–1071 – Resistance in the East

It was in this year that William faced his greatest threat, and this came from the Danish King Sweiyn who pulled together an army to conquer England. The Danish army hoped to ignite the Northern Rebellion again with their assistance, but there was not enough appetite to do so. However, William considered the threat to be enough that he paid a massive fortune for them to leave. Some of these Danes only moved south to join forces with another rebellion being led by Hereward the Wake. Hereward, just like Eadric, conducted guerrilla like operations from the safety of his base on the Isle of Ely. It would be a long time before William could subdue this resistance.

William's Death Bed Confession

Although we cannot be certain that William did indeed say this, it was however recorded by the Chronicler Orderic Vitalis that when William died, he had stated:

> *'I've persecuted the natives of England beyond all reason, whether gentle or simple. I have cruelly oppressed them and unjustly disinherited them, killed innumerable multitudes by famine or the sword and become the barbarous murderer of many thousands both young and old of that fine race of people.'*

Given this, by his own confession… William was a tyrant of immense magnitude to the people of England.

The Search begins….

When looking into the locations where Robin would frequent, I wanted to get a copy of one of the earliest maps of Nottinghamshire. There was a particular reason for this too. The earliest detailed maps of the counties of the United Kingdom were done by the Tudor Cartographer – Christopher Saxton (c. 1542 to c. 1610). His work gave rise to a new standard for map making in the country and for succeeding maps for over a hundred years later. He is also referred to as the 'Father of English Cartography'. In 1574 Christopher was commissioned to survey the country, partly financed by Queen Elizabeth, a huge undertaking at the time, however it was achieved in record time by 1578. He was also accompanied by his brother Robert Saxton as a fellow surveyor. Initial county sheets were issued leading up to the introduction of an '*Atlas of the Counties of England and Wales*' in 1579. This was the first ever atlas of England and Wales, something of vital importance and significance. John Speed (c. 1551 – 1629) used Saxton's maps as a blueprint for his own, only building on them with a bit more detail.

The Saxton Map of Nottinghamshire shown here is from 1607 and then following, a close-up image showing the surrounding area to Nottingham, including Sherwood Forest.

Above and below: Christopher Saxton's map of Nottinghamshire (surveyed circa 1590), with close reference to Sherwood Forest.

The reason why I mention Christopher Saxton, other than recording the first detailed map of Nottinghamshire, is due to my own family links. On my mother's side, her maiden name was Saxton – the surname literally means the person comes from a 'Saxon settlement'. My mother also believed that her side of the family traced back to Christopher Saxton, but this needed to be researched further. So, this will possibly be one of my jobs for the future. It is also worth noting that my Grandfather – Harry Saxton, served at the end of the First World War with the Royal Flying Corps (later Fleet Air Arms) and he was, according to my mother, the first pilot to fly over the German Fleet surrendering at Scapa Flow at the end of the war – and this included taking famous pictures of the event. Here is a picture of him.

Above: Harry Saxton.

So, my own interest in both the Saxton name and historical reference to earlier times is probably very evident here. But that is the beauty in bringing history to life, we are still connected in some way.... be it via just our surname or by more deeper ancestral links.

It was also, only towards the completion of writing this book, that another blast from the past hit me. Again, on my mother's side, my grandmother's maiden surname was Greene, and her father (my Great Grandfather) was George Washington Greene. I have been told that ancestrally, there might be a link (but uncertain exactly how far back this is, but in all honesty, there appears to be a bit of a resemblance there) to none other than Richard Greene! If you are not familiar with who Richard Greene was, like myself, it will come as a bit of a shock, as it certainly did to me. But Richard Greene was a famous Robin Hood actor from the 1950's and 60's. He was the star in the film 'The Sword of Sherwood' (1960) and starred in 143 individual episodes of the TV series 'The Adventures of Robin Hood' (from 1955 to 1959). I will be following up upon this, guaranteed. Naturally this is way before my time, but is that just some sort of a coincidence? Maybe, but it is funny how these things can happen!

Now, back to looking for the 'real' Robin Hood. So, when talking about Nottingham, it is recognised as a Saxon settlement which was based upon a chieftain called 'Snod' or 'Snot' and was referred to as Snotingham in old English. Over time, luckily, the name was shortened to the name we know today. But at the time that Christopher Saxton created this map, the name was Nottingham. But we can appreciate from this point alone that names can change over time and the way in which they are pronounced would influence the way in which they were written and until we had standardised English, then their spellings could be very varied, yet sound similar. This point will become more apparent later on.

It is also worth noting the name 'Sherwood Forest' originates from the term 'Shire' meaning the county, so the forest of the county. Were there any other forests named 'woods of the shire' at this time, by name or by nature?

Nottingham in 1680.—P. 119.

William's Legacy

They say that history is written by the victorious and I think most people can relate to that, however how do you evaluate that concept? Is it by what is written in history books, by the long-lasting changes they made to society, or is it by how long the legacy of the person recording their history lasts? Or is it securing their bloodline? With William the Conqueror, the Duke that became a King, how long did his legacy last? And what was his legacy to the people that he once controlled? Well, it has to be said that his influence on the British people was profound, a new feudal system was introduced, abolishing slavery, introducing forest law, the Domesday Book, building an extensive network of castles around the country, introducing some French/Norman language and customs to the people and stretching his sphere of influence across the channel to lands held in Normandy. Yet, upon William's death in September, 1087 he had left behind a dis-jointed England, with the last Anglo Saxon rebellion being suppressed in 1075 (Revolt of the Earls) and then, following his death, a warring rebellion between two of his sons - William Rufus (William II – 'Rufus being Latin for 'the Red' – possibly due to having red hair) and Robert Curthose fighting over the lands held between England and Normandy. Note: William's second eldest son, Richard, had died on a hunting trip in 1075 within the New Forest.

William, on his deathbed, had reluctantly given the control of Normandy to the eldest, exiled and most arrogant son, Robert Curthose, which now divided the states of England and Normandy. William II won the rebellions in order to secure the throne of England and Henry I (the youngest son of William I – Henry Beauclerc) inherited the throne following the death of William II. Again, William II was killed in a hunting accident in the New Forest (believed to be near Brokenhurst) in August 1100 by an arrow piercing his lungs. Henry I had married Matilda (daughter of Macolm III of Scotland) at Westminster Abbey in November 1100 – it is known that Matilda was originally called Edith and was a member of the West Saxon Royal Family (the niece of Edgar Ætheling (a former contender to the English throne following the death of Edward the Confessor), and this was seen as a political alliance that will help unify the country and give further legitimacy to the throne. Due to troubles in Normandy, Henry mounted excursions into Normandy as it was said the Duke of Normandy, Robert Curthose

(Curthose meaning 'short stockings' a name given to him by his father), had not honoured some of the previous treaties made. Between 1103 and 1106 battles took place between the different sides with a decisive battle in September 1106 at Tinchebray Castle, Normandy. Duke Robert was taken prisoner and Henry, having no powers to remove the Duke's title, remained as Guardian of the Dutchy instead. Now was the question of who is the rightful successor to the Duchy of Normandy? Henry tried to persuade the King of France – Louis VI, that the rightful heir should be his son, Wiliam Adedlin, yet despite initial successful negotiations involving vast sums of money, Louis decided with someone else, William Clito. War broke out between the two sides and this was only resolved by the dealings with Pope Callixtus II, who told them that they need to seek peace and reconcile their differences. In June 1120, this was eventually achieved in Henry's favour by his son, William Adedlin, paying homage to King Philip in return for Philip's agreement to William's rights to the Duchy. However, this was short lived as on the 25th of November, 1120, Henry left the harbour of Barfleur for England leaving his son to follow later on in a ship called the 'White ship'. Both crew and passengers were drunk, and the ship hit a submerged rock just outside the harbour, killing all but one person on board.

This left the succession open to dispute, as Henry had now lost his only legitimate son. In an attempt to overcome this, he re-married. Henry, now the age of around 54, married an attractive 18 year old lady called Adeliza of Louvain at Windsor Castle in January, 1121. Unfortunately, despite the marriage being successful, Henry and Adeliza did not conceive any children, so Henry would have been worried about his dynasty and the heir that he should now leave. Henry did have illegitimate children including a son, Robert FitzRoy, Earl of Gloucester, however this would not have looked favourably with English traditions and customs. So, he started to look towards his nephews, one of which was Stephen of Blois and Henry arranged a marriage between Stephen and a wealthy noble lady Matilda, Countess of Boulogne.

Henry I died on December 1st, 1135 and his corpse was taken to Rouen where it was embalmed with his entrails buried locally at the priory of Notre-Dame du Pré and the remaining body was taken to England and interred at Reading Abbey.

So, the direct bloodline to the throne from William the Conqueror was now extinguished, it had lasted only 69 years in total.

However....

The scene had already been set for the emergence of a hero.
An Anglo-Saxon hero. One whose name now echoes around the
World, and throughout history…..

Above: Robin and his band of Merry Men in the Greenwood.

Introduction

Robin Hood. Sherwood Forest. Little John. Maid Marion, Friar Tuck, the Sheriff of Nottingham. We are all familiar with the names and the storyline. We have grown up watching or reading about Robin's exploits. He is a national hero, even an international hero. An outlaw but one with principles! We respect him for taking on the oppressive Norman Elite during the Middle Ages. He was a Saxon of noble birth (or maybe, just a Yeoman (middle class/trades-person)) who has his lands removed from him following his return from the Crusades. He has absolute loyalty to the King but has issue with the local Sheriff and seeks shelter within the mystical Sherwood Forest. He takes, with his band of 'Merry Men', from the rich (and, might I add, the corrupt Church) and then gives to the poor. He falls in love with Maid Marion. He saves the Kingdom from a rebellion by Prince John and is pardoned by the King (Richard) for his outlaw antics. Wow... what a story! We love it... it represents a heroic tale of a freedom fighter with moral values and basically, enacting the fight between good and evil. It has turned into the most famous folklore tale from England, and it has given our nation an heirloom from a bygone Anglo-Saxon period. The ballads handed down through the generations were initially orally told and then around 30 years after the development of the printing press (William Caxton – late 1470's) were we given 'A Guest of Robin Hode' (c. 1500). This is the first printed version of his stories and a blast from our past....

So, that was a very quick outline of what we know about Robin Hood. But was it right?

Hundreds of books have been written about him, and I stress that - **hundreds of books!** Scholars have trawled through the records, stretching as far back to the Doomsday Book, in order to trace this incredible person. But have all those hours of time been wasted? That's the question. So, what do we know? Let's start from the beginning:

Is Robin Hood just a Fairytale, or a Myth? This is clearly a 'No'.... just like the tales of King Arthur, it is considered to be a 'Legend' due to historical links to 'believed' actual people who once lived. These stories have been told, re-told and no doubt altered and exaggerated over the hundreds of years. Indeed, even today you can appreciate this... consider the films Robin Hood: Prince of Thieves (1991) with Kevin Costner and Robin Hood (2010) with Russell Crowe and how these storylines of Robin have changed considerably in the space of 20 years. So, we know and understand that the narrative to Robin Hood and his stories have changed dramatically over the many centuries... mostly, due to the audience that it was aimed at. Some of the characters associated with the legend are relative newcomers appearing over 200 years later – such as the important figure of Maid Marion – first appearing in the late 16th Century.

So, let's have a very brief and quick look at the main contenders for the title of Robin Hood:

Robert Hod of York

Records from 1226 confirm that his possessions of 32 shillings and 6 pence were confiscated due to monies owed to St. Peter's in York, and he became an outlaw. The following year he was called 'Hobbehod'. It is understood that this Robert/Robin was the earliest Robin to be known as an outlaw. There is very limited correlation with the actual Robin Hood stories, other than a name and becoming an outlaw.

Robin Hood of Wakefield

A Robert Hood was identified as living in Wakefield during the early decades of the 14th Century and was later living within the local forests of Yorkshire. Information is limited.

Robyn Hod

A Robyn Hode was recorded as being employed by Edward II of England in 1323. This was linked to the idea that Robyn had been a rebel who had been defeated at the Battle of Boroughbridge in 1322, but there are considered problems with this, as new research appears to point towards Robyn was already in the Kings service before this point in time. Therefore, there is limited correlation with the actual Robin Hood.

Robin of Loxley

Loxley is a village in South Yorkshire, near Sheffield, however there is no evidence of any Robin Hood being associated with this particular place.

Robert Fitzooth/Earl of Huntingdon

Robert Fitzooth (1160–1247) was first mentioned to be associated with Robin Hood and the Earl of Huntingdon that was first published in William Stukeley's 'Paleographica Britannica' in 1746. It is understood that Stukeley, innocently or purposefully, confused the family name Fitzooth and Fitz Odo, (Lord of Loxley Manor in Warwickshire), from the reign of Richard I to Henry II. The name 'Fitz' refers to the illegitimate nature of the 'son of'. Fitz Odo was therefore understood to have been associated with Bishop Odo, half-brother of William the Conqueror, so clearly of Norman descent. There are many adaptations regarding this character, with tenuous links to another member of the family in order to fill in gaps, and even ideas that Stukeley was forging documents in order to fit the narrative, but it is agreed that there are limitations to the historical character of Robin Hood. It is because of this character, that most Robin Hood stories are placed in the period of Richard I.

An Alias

One of the convincing ideas is that Robin Hood was an alias. The first recorded mention of a stock name for an outlaw was in 1262 in Berkshire, where the surname of 'Robehod' was given to a man because he had been outlawed. This is quite telling, as it would appear to indicate that the Robin Hood legend was already well established by the mid-13th Century and the term of 'Robehod' or 'Robin Hood' was collectively used as some sort of outlaw.

Basically, there is not a lot to go on…..

So, given the expanse of time, the number of different and knowledgeable people who have looked into this legend... what can I possibly offer to this debate? Well, I hope you can join me on this journey as we delve into the past and look for clues ourselves.... but first things first, an experiment. I want you to put this book down for a minute and just do a quick internet search for images of a 'hooded person'.

Interesting? Now, that is our own modern day take upon what is the representation of a hooded person. Would our medieval predecessors have shared that same idea? I am guessing so. We will come back to this later in the book.

But Robin Hood is a person with a surname. Correct? Well, it was in the Medieval period that people first decided upon the need for surnames, and this is where we get the basis for a lot of our modern-day family names. Names such as Smith, Knight, Taylor, Cook, Turner and many more – including Glover might I add, are all based upon the trade or occupation they once held. Names such as Swift, Armstrong, Strong, Longfellow, White, Short relate to personal attributes they might have had, other names such as Hill, Dale, Wood, York, Sutton, Lancaster relate to the location that they came from. And names such as Johnson, Harrison, Richardson refer to 'son of' and to add to this are some Welsh names such as Jones – that also follow the same pattern here. So, the surname itself helps give a bit of potential background to the person they represented, or their potential background. So was Hood related to a clothing/hood tradesperson.... or to an attribute? Let's look at the name with a bit more context.

Above: A 'hooded person' (the author) at nighttime next to one of his research locations.

The Name

We all know the name, we are all familiar with the stories, it has certainly become part of the fabric that makes up the British Heritage. Yet not being restricted to the British Isles, if you also mention his name, then he is known about around the world. Why would this be? This ancient set of stories that reverberate around the centuries and the world. But before we start looking at the history, what was his true name? We have Robin Hood, Robert Hod, Robyn Hode, Robehod, Robyne Hude, Robert Hoode, Hoods, Hude, Hud, Hudd and others... so which one is most accurate? Well, in essence, they all are! In the Middle Ages, it was common for typical Anglo-Saxon names to be characterised by many different spellings – basically, the English Language had not become 'standardised' yet. Shakespeare, over 200 years later, was also yet to invent over 1,700 English words (up until his death in 1616). So, you can see, the English language was still developing for well over 300 years following the earliest references to Robin Hood. You can now see why this is such a detective story. Many, many scholars have looked and tried their best to trace the original character from the history books. However, the English language itself is made up of Old English, Latin, French, Danish, Norse plus a few extra languages being incorporated into its development. As well as the non- standardised spelling of words, referring to early documents including Robin has proved difficult and so an element of translation has been necessary. And to cap it all, Robin Hood's name might just be an alias to another name! This is going to be a tough nut to crack!

That said, future documents from this period may yet surface and offer glimpses into the true origins of this legend, but for now, we must look at what is currently available.

The origins to the Legend

Above: Robin Hood, together with Maid Marion, as portrayed in 16-17th century. A dashing figure and very different to the way we visualise him today.

Through the ages there have been many stories about the exploits of Robin Hood. So how do you know which of these is closer to the truth? We know that over the years the stories have been altered and additional parts and characters added. This has served well in keeping the legend alive... but we do know that the stories are tailored to the audience of the time. Just take a look at this image of Robin Hood from the 1600's – very different to how he would have dressed originally. During the period we are looking at, there is no literary evidence, so the stories would have been based upon oral traditions. The first written ballad was 'Robin Hood and the Monk' – a sole surviving written manuscript from around 1450 (around 250 years after the understood period in question) and then printed records appear very shortly after the invention of the printing press – with the 'A Geste of Robyn Hode' printed in around 1500 – although the text itself is estimated to have been compiled around 1450. So, the earliest references would most likely have been based upon oral stories that have been passed down through the ages, spread by word of mouth to different parts of the country. Clearly there was every opportunity for the tales to be inflated, altered or subjected to a case of Chinese Whispers. We all know how the human mind works and stories are directly tailored to the audience they appeal to. Tales grow longer the more they are told! So, yes, quite a Legend we are trying to solve here based upon very limited factual evidence.

All that said, where do we start in this search? I have read many books about the 'true origins' of Robin Hood – Robert of Loxley, Robin Longstride, Robert Earl of Huntingdon, they all come up with very different characters from recorded history with tenuous links to the fabled character. Is one of these correct or are all of them correct? Just like the spellings of the name, has different real life characters all played their part into the development of the stories that we know and cherish today? So, with that thought, where do we start?

OK, I am now going to ask you, the reader, a question. Many of you will know the answer to this, some will be faced with a paradox situation. So let me just ask you the question.... What came first – the Chicken or the Egg? Profound? Ponder on it for a while.... Can I give you a clue to help answer this one.... when I say (like I have done many times in the past) – it's a fish! Confused? Good. If you have never tried to answer this age-old question then me saying it was a fish will add even more confusion, so let me explain. We know that chickens come from eggs, but a chicken (a type of jungle fowl) is a bird and all birds lay eggs – correct? Now where did birds evolve from? As we now know, they developed or evolved as an offshoot from Dinosaurs, and we also know that Dinosaurs all laid eggs... and where did Dinosaurs evolve from? Well, they came from Reptiles, and reptiles come from Amphibians and amphibians evolved from fish – and we know that fish etc. all lay eggs – correct? Now, we can go back further in time, but the principle is that we can see the evolution of the egg much further back in time than that of the chicken. That is to say, the egg comes first by at least 500 million years! So, what is my point here?

OK, let's look at where we should focus our attention. Rather than going around in circles looking at possible links to people mentioned in the stories behind the earliest ballads (Robin Hood and the Monk - written in the 1450's, and later

Geste of Robyn Hode, circa 1500 ('Geste' meaning tale or adventure), then just like the chicken and egg paradox, we should look back to the earliest reference to Robin Hood and examine that more thoroughly and this takes us back to 1377 - 'The Vision of Piers Plowman' by William Langland.

This piece of literary work was written in the shadows of the Black Death (in England this lasted from June 1348 to December 1349). It is recognised as one of the greatest poems from the English Middle Ages and may well have influenced the later writings of Chaucer's Canterbury Tales. It basically follows the visions revealed in dreams by a person called 'Will' whilst asleep 'one May morning in the Malvern Hills'. The story follows that Will was trying to find an elusive farmhand who can teach him how to live a good Christian life, yet with a background of revealing the sinful ways of the late medieval people of this time. There were certainly some moral lessons to be learnt by the reader, yet William Langland, the author, included humour at times to underline serious points. The seven deadly sins appear to Will in the form of characters – Gluttony is represented by a rich knight and Sloth is an incompetent priest. They all seek forgiveness from a figure called 'Repentance' due to a sermon delivered by a character called 'Reason'. Reason, who acted as an archbishop, was preaching to the Kingdom of the sinful ways of its people and preached the plague was God's punishment. The significance of Langland's manuscript would have been immense at this time, acting as a moral compass, indeed, during the Peasants Revolt (1381), one of its leaders – John Ball (a priest) used characters from Piers Plowman in his communications, writings and speeches (often with rhyme) which he used to justify attacks on the established church, rich merchants and nobility.

Ball was a very vocal member of the clergy which brought him into conflict with the hierarchy of the Church and the Archbishop of Canterbury, Simon of Sudbury. Thrown into prison on several occasions, he was released by Kentish rebels prior to the Peasants Revolt. The following is part of a speech he gave at Blackheath, near Greenwich (the Peasant's Revolt rendezvous point) prior to their march on London.

> *'When Adam delved and Eve span, Who was then the gentleman. From the beginning all men by nature were created alike, and our bondage or servitude came in by the unjust oppression of naughty men. For if God would have had any bondmen from the beginning, He would have appointed who should be bond, and who free. And therefore I exhort you to consider that now the time is come, appointed to us by God, in which ye may (if ye will) cast off the yoke of bondage, and recover liberty.'*

The Revolt ultimately failed. King Richard II initially agreed to the demands of the 100,000 rebels present – in essence 'We will be free forever, our heirs and our lands' – yet in a face to face meeting with Wat Tyler, the other leader, there became a heated scuffle and the Mayor of London (Sir William Walworth) stabbed Wat through the throat and upon assurances of forgiveness from the King, the revolt dispersed. Forgiveness was not granted to all, Ball was later taken prisoner at Coventry and after trial, he was hung, drawn and quartered at St. Albans in the presence of the King on 15th July, 1381. His head was displayed on a pike at London Bridge and the four parts of his body were displayed at four different towns as a warning to others.

You can appreciate now how powerful Langland's story was. Did it play a part in the inspiration behind the Peasant's Revolt? Possibly, but it certainly had some level of influence upon one of the leaders – John Ball. So... what has this got to do with Robin Hood? Well, Robin Hood's name appears when Will, in search of the Plowman, meets 'Sloth' – the incompetent priest – where Sloth states:

'If this was my dying day, I still couldn't be bothered to keep awake. I don't even know the Paternoster (from Latin pater noster: 'Our Father' – referring to the Lord's prayer) perfectly, not as a priest should really sing it. I know plenty of ballads about Robin Hood and Randolph, Earl of Chester, but I don't know a verse about our Lord or our Lady'.

Is this it? Just this one liner that suggests that the inept priest knows more detail about the stories of Robin Hood than he does about his clerical requirements. Yes, this is it. But what is clear is that Robin was a well-known character at this time, more popular maybe than the teachings from the Church. Don't you think that this is interesting? This book about moral values of the time, picking fault with the corruption and flaws of the Church (and nobles) suggesting that Robin Hood was more popular. You have seen the above results of Piers Plowman to the populace, how it likely affected John Ball resulting in stirring up the feelings of the injustices of the late Medieval Period. Considering the earliest known ballad is the 15th Century 'Robin Hood and the Monk' (housed at Cambridge University), it is understood to have been written after 1450 and contains the earliest elements between Robin and the local Sheriff of Nottingham. This certainly helps paint the picture of the person we recognise in our modern stories, but still we are none the wiser who Robin really was. I just want to add that this first ballad recorded is around 73 years following Piers Plowman.

There is, however, another reference written by Andrew de Wyntoun (c.1350-c.1423), a Scottish Augustinian clergyman and, at the request of his patron Sir John of Wemyss, he wrote *'The Orgynale Cronykil of Scotland'* - Chronicles of

Scotland. This comprised of the history of Scotland from mythical times through to the accession of James I of Scotland in 1406. It is understood that this Chronicle was written/completed by the year 1420, and it places the below passage with its historical record linking Robin to between the years 1283 and 1285.

> Than litill Iohne and Robyne Hude
> Waichmen were commendit gud,
> In Yngilwode and Bernysdale
> And usit this tyme thar travale

Translated as:

> Little John and Robin Hude
> As forest outlaws were well renowned
> In Inglewood and Barnsdale
> All this time they plied their trade.

This is helpful by linking a date to the reign of Edward 1st. This also links in with the early ballads that mention King Edward – 'Our comely King'. However, scholars think this King relates to Edward III. Yet popular culture places Robin earlier, at the time of Richard the Lionheart, and when the country was under the influence and misrule of his bad brother John – this was whilst Richard was on the third Crusade to the Holy Lands. There is also a link here to Barnsdale in Yorkshire (Bernysdale – notice the difference between Medieval and modern-day spellings), rather than Nottingham or Sherwood. So, with this all-in mind I have drawn up a list of the Kings (including the brief reign of Empress Matilda), in order to see what we are up against.

Medieval Kings (and an Empress) of England from the time of the Norman Conquest through to when Robin Hood was first mentioned.

- **Edward the Confessor, 1042 to 1066**
- **King Harold II, 1066**
- **King William I, the Conqueror, 1066 to 1087**
- **King William II, Rufus, 1087 to 1100**
- **King Henry I, 1100 to 1135**
- **King Stephen, 1135 to 1141**
- **Empress Matilda, 1141 to 1142** (brief period due to a rebellion)
- **King Stephen, 1142 to 1154** (returned to the throne)
- **King Henry II, 1154 to 1189**

- **King Richard I, Lionheart, 1189 to 1199**
- **King John, Lackland, 1199 to 1216**
- **King Henry III, 1216 to 1272**
- **Edward I, The Hammer of the Scots, 1272 to 1307**
- **Edward II, 1307 to 1327**
- **Edward III, 1327 to 1377**
- **Richard II, 1377 to 1399**
- **Henry IV, 1399 to 1413**

So, the period we are looking at comprises of at least 188 years (1189 through to 1377). What's more, there are no actual historical accounts that the person ever existed, was ever met by someone, or events recorded of his activities. Don't you think that is strange for such a famous person, who was admired by the common people and written about in rhyming ballads throughout the years? Many scholars have tried to trace the person to the legend and have come up with nothing or very tenuous outcomes.

Now, did the likes of Piers Plowman's moral stories influence and shape the development of later stories surrounding Robin Hood and the ones that we know and appreciate today? Did the lessons learnt from the Peasant's Revolt and the people rising up against the tyranny of the Norman nobility mean that previous ballads about this famous character morphed a local folklore tale into stories to suit a new audience? All we know is that there is no evidence who was the real Robin Hood. We have seen how the stories changed over time, with new characters being added to the storyline and with new adventures. It seems like this Legend will never be solved. If that is the case, why am I writing this book? Well, if you have read my previous book, you will understand that sometimes mysteries can be solved, but it won't be quite how you imagine it be. You may also recall that I had previously referenced Robin Hood (Page 152) with links to the Green Man..... so, let's take another look at this larger-than-life character from 'Merrie Olde England!'

Above: Robin Hood being defeated by Little John crossing the river.

The Stories

First of all, I want you to think of a few films that you have previously watched. I think that you will find that most will follow a predictable storyline... after a brief introduction about the background/leading characters, then there is drama, bad things happen, we get the appearance of the Villain, there is then basically a fight between good and evil and with the ending of the film, the good guys are triumphant. Then end titles appear and you feel happy – you have just been preached a moral lesson of good over bad. Yes, when you look it that way, they are predictable. How many films have you watched where there isn't a happy ending? Even with horror films, many people might die but the main character will end up surviving to escape and warn others. This is how the human psyche works when it comes to our entertainment. We don't want to leave the cinema feeling bad or sad... we want to leave on a high! Is that not true of the Robin Hood films? Does the bad Sheriff of Nottingham meet his karma? Would that have been the way that stories and plays would have performed in Merrie Olde England? So, with that in mind, let us see the earliest ballad of Robin... Robin Hood and the Monk.

The story starts off with Little John talking of the May morning, however Robin is unhappy because he cannot attend Mass or martins (a church service held in the morning, usually whilst still dark), however he decides to go to a service in Nottingham (linked to his devotion to the Vrigin Mary). He is advised by 'Moche' (Much, the Miller's son) to take some men with him, at least 12 of them, however he refuses and only goes by himself with Little John. On his journey to Nottingham, he makes a bet with Little John, which he loses and refuses to pay his dues because they cannot agree on a mutual sum. So Little John leaves him at this point.

By himself, Robin goes to St. Mary's Church in Nottingham and prays. There he is seen by a Monk that Robin had previously robbed, and the Monk goes and warns the Sheriff. The Sheriff then arrives with a lot of soldiers and attempt to arrest him. Robin is seen fighting them off wielding a two-handed sword, wounding many and killing 12 of the Sheriffs men. During this skirmish, Robin's sword breaks, so he runs into the Church trying to evade capture.

Unfortunately, there is a page missing from the ballad at this point, which would indicate that Robin is actually captured and then the news of his capture reaching his men. There is confusion, but Little John takes the initiative and decides on a rescue attempt. Robin's band of men capture the Monk who was riding past, accompanied by his page. Little John shows no mercy and kills the Monk for informing the Sheriff, and Much kills the page boy, so that no one can tell of their actions. They find letters meant for the King within the Monk's possessions.

Little John comes up with a plan and goes with Much to the King (the actual King is not mentioned here) and takes the letters with him. Little John explains to the King that the Monk had died on the way, but wanted the letters to be delivered to him. The King appreciates this and gives the visitors gifts, and orders to bring Robin Hood to him directly. Little John takes the orders to the Sheriff and explains to him that the Monk is not with them as the King had made him an Abbott. They make their way to the prison, where they kill the jailer, and promptly escape with Robin.

Robin is grateful for Little John's actions and offers to be led by him, yet Little John disagrees and still wants Robin to lead him and the band of men. Back in Nottingham, the Sheriff dares not face the King. As for the King, he is angry that he had been fooled yet admits that Little John must be the most 'loyal man in England' and given that they had fooled everyone, then the matter was dropped.

Outlaw

We know that in the acknowledged stories, Robin Hood is classed as an 'outlaw' and in the adventures this involved Robin stealing from the rich and corrupt clergy to give to the poor. Is this the actions of the typical outlaw of the time, or is it a story with hidden principles and the acts of a very noble person? So, let's look at the term 'outlaw' itself – does this literally just mean a thief? Well, no. In the first sense, 'Outlaw' basically means that the person is **'declared as outside the protection of the law'**. In Robin Hood's day, this concept probably originated from Roman Law - *Homo sacer* (Latin for "the sacred man" or 'the accursed man') – however, early Roman religion refers to *sacer* denoting anything as being 'set apart' from common society and, also encompasses both the sense of 'hallowed' (definition: greatly revered and honoured) and that of 'cursed' (ill-fated). So, meaning they are basically considered 'outside of the law' in some way. This is interesting in relation to what we will look at later. There is also a secondary meaning of 'Outlaw', in that a person systematically avoids capture by evading or hiding from the law or by using other means, like violence to prevent capture.

So, when we look at the term 'outlaw' we understand what this means, but in Robin Hood's Day, this might be a reference to something quite different. Was he just a thief then? Ponder on that.

Modern day outlaws?

Can we see any modern-day examples of people rebelling against perceived unjust taxes and acting 'outside of the law'? Well, the ULEZ scheme (Outer London air quality measures) being rolled out despite popular opinion being against this, as it is seen as a heavy tax on poorer people when there was limited or conflicting evidence pointing towards poor air quality. There are people referred to as modern day 'Robin Hood's' that are indeed 'hooded' and responsible for the destruction of many of the operating cameras. Are these truly modern-day Robin Hoods? Are they thieves? Is the Mayor of London an unjust person in authority on par with the Sheriff of Nottingham? You be the judge, but you can appreciate where the term Robin Hood is used in context for standing up to perceived unjust acts of authority.

What do the academics say?

During my research I came across a very well-presented lecture by Stephen Church, Professor of Medieval History at the University of East Anglia. I also love the fact that he presented this on the 1st. May 2018. I thoroughly recommend that you watch this lecture, which is recorded on Youtube (Gresham College Lecture: In Search of the Medieval Outlaw: The Tales of Robin Hood). This is a person who has taken the time to study this period and sets the scene for the direction we are going to take later in this book. I will quote his opening statement here, together with the content from his first presentation slide:

> 'I would like to begin this lecture with a bold statement about Robin Hood's identity. There is absolutely no evidence whatsoever that there was a physical person called Robin Hood, who is the progenitor of our mythical Robin Hood. Neither have the most diligent archivists nor the most inventive historian has been able to find him, yet despite this fact Robin Hood still has a place in the definitive Oxford Dictionary of National Biographies – and here is the start of what they have to say about him: -
>
> - Over 60,000 biographies, 72 million words, 11,000 portraits of signify. (Oxford Dictionary of National Biography)
> - Hood, Robin (supp. fl. Late 12th–13th cent.), legendary outlaw hero, is wellnigh impossible to identify, first because of the sparsity and peculiar nature of the evidence, and second because Robin quickly became a composite figure of an archetypal criminal, and then an outlaw hero. Cant, influential or notorious figures who shaped British History. (J.C Holt, ODNB).'

In summary, what else was mentioned?

Well, unlike King Arthur who had at least some form of literary record, due to the legends appealing to nobility of the time, Robin was a man of the people, he was one of the people and therefore would have been restricted to the taverns and markets of the day, so no literary records are available until much later in time. It also needs to be stressed that he appealed to the common people of the day – this would have been the native Anglo-Saxon people. As a result, it would have been oral tales that led to the later printed versions that we now know today. Stephen then explains some of the stories related to the legends. The different types of Robin, through the Gest of Robin Hood and later stories together with the early references made, such as Piers Plowman. Even within the Gest of Robin Hood, there are different distinct types of Robin, yet there were many more as time goes by. The narrative changes all the time.

There was an interesting reference to a 13th Century manuscript from Lincoln Cathedral. It was believed that a schoolboy had written a piece of graffiti upon it in Latin in the form of a poem that has been translated as:

'*Robin Hood in Sherwood stood, hooded, hatted, hosed and shod, four and twenty arrows held in his hand'*

It is believed that this graffiti dated back to sometime in the 15th Century.

This helps to confirm the fragility of the evidence that we have from this period, but this single piece of graffiti confirms that there was already an oral tradition in poem form for Robin, which certainly appealed to 'bored schoolboys'! It also links Robin with Sherwood Forest, which is noted as lacking from the early versions of the stories, which points towards Yorkshire.

It is noted that until the 16th Century, Robin appealed to the lower classes of society (being initially a yeoman) and only when he was re-cast as a knight returning from the crusades (only to find that he has lost his lands to the Sheriff) that he was then also cherished by the upper class.

Stephen did not believe there was an actual person related to the Legend. Stephen then thinks the best way to describe Robin Hood as a Time Lord – just like Dr Who. Many Dr's have come and gone, but the Dr still remains very appropriate to the current generation – because the stories are altered to appease the audience. This, I feel, is a particularly good analogy of what has happened in the past, right the way through to the present. The original stories, orally told, have been altered throughout time and then when it came to these oral records being written, they are very, very different to the original events. But by the same token, there must have been an original Dr Who that started the saga.

Now the bit that Stephen did cover, I am more interested in: Reference to Robin Hood being associated with the May Day Games was of significance. When looking into this, references were only found in May Day Celebrations in Southern England, Southwest England, and one reference within East Anglia, plus Scotland (which was a separate kingdom at this time). The places lacking reference included Wales and Northern England – most importantly, no mention in Yorkshire or Nottinghamshire – where you would have expected. Yet clearly, Robin was associated with the activities of the May Games, indeed, there was also an actual Robin Hood's Day in places at this time, which may or may not have coincided with the actual May Day itself.

At these celebrations, Robin was the Lord of Misrule, a symbol of fertility who was specially selected for his youth and abilities. Archery competitions, rough and tumble antics, plays and rowdy games were then held. Robin, in association with his team of 'Merry Men' (the more the merrier), would go around collecting money for worthy causes and for the Church, sometimes using very persuasive methods. May Day was a wild day, with lots of drinking and dancing – indeed its exactly why it was called the Merry, Merry Month of May!

Don't you think that this is strange? An outlaw celebrated with the festivals for the coming of Summer? But like all good stories, there must be a reason for this and that is the direction this book will take us.

Historical References

Let's start to think outside of the box now.

With this idea, we are going to go on an adventure, travelling back in time, to be precise, we are going back to the Mesolithic period and to North Yorkshire. A location initially discovered in 1947 by an amateur archaeologist, Jonn Moore, gives us a snapshot in time to a bygone age – the place is called Star Carr. This historical location has been uniquely preserved by the silts and muds that covered this middle stone age set of lakeside settlements. It dates back over 11,000 years. How is this important to Robin Hood? Well, first of all, it should be noted that the earliest preserved bow (and micro arrowheads) in the world has been discovered here. The bow itself was made from a willow tree. There are earlier references of bow and arrows being used, the earliest believed stone arrowheads were found in South Africa at sites like Sibudu cave, which dates back to around 60,000 years ago. However, as you will appreciate, preservation over time of wooden objects is more unlikely the further you go back in time, yet the preservation process seen at Star Carr is exceptional, as the wooden frames to house structures are well represented together with all sorts of tools and implements hidden within different sections of the homes – including this bow!

OK, so that is an interesting piece of information, yet has little to do with the subject of this book. Correct, maybe, yet also incorrect! As, also, within the walls of these dwellings were located red deer skulls with eye holes and leather strap attachments. These were understood to have been used as ceremonial head dresses. So based upon these ornamental costumes we get a glimpse into the mindset and religious practices of our ancestors. Yes, 11,000 years ago, our ancestors were dressed up wearing deer scalps, and likely covered also in deer pelts, as, we can only guess, as a means of a religious practice. You can start to imagine the scenes where these people would dance around campfires dressed as deer and partaking in celebrations or religious rites. Why would this be? Why would these bygone people be doing such antics? Ponder for a moment and think about that.

You can now appreciate that the people of this time were very connected to their natural surroundings. They would not have understood how the world works, i.e.

in the same way as we do **(well, I say that, but within our own current limitations)**. They would have been very superstitious, and I stress that, what they saw that they did not understand would have affected them greatly in the way that they thought and behaved. No doubt red deer made up some of their daily diet, so does that automatically mean that they should worship these creatures? Should these deer become part of their religion? Well, we can see some of the traditions of more modern-day native tribes and how they are connected, including reaching out to the 'spirit world', which included the spirits of the animals. Now, could there be some other kind of driving force behind their beliefs? That is the question that no scientist or archaeologist has thought of to date, yet that is something we will look at later. In our eyes, what we are seeing here is the birth of a belief system, in fact, a type of religion.

Now we will try and bring some of this together.

Fertility

This is where we have to cast away our modern-day ideas and think more like our earlier ancestors, who had, compared to us, very limited understandings of the world that they lived in. As man moved away from a nomadic hunter gatherer lifestyle to a more static farming tradition, then the emergence of means to calculate the growing seasons become evident. Stonehenge pays testament to that fact, and we still witness some of the ceremonies every summer and winter solstice that keeps those ancient traditions alive. Man was starting to move away from the day-to-day existence of foraging for food, to now predicting when to sow and harvest crops and you will appreciate that these occasions became a time of great celebration (or, of trepidation). A celebration of the summertime and also, with regards to the winter solstice, a time to celebrate the turning point of the sun along the horizon and when the daylight hours will start to get longer. Christmas has a very real link with that, which is covered better in my previous book.

You will appreciate then, given the manner in which people were starting to think, understanding the seasons was very, very important, including when to plant crops. This did not just extend to the different kind of crops; this would also relate to feelings linked to domesticated animals and humans alike. Things like when sheep and cattle could mate in order to bare offspring at the right time the following year. For example, with sheep, you will appreciate this because they are all born in the springtime, and that is no coincidence. You can also only imagine how tough life was in these bygone days. With average life expectancy being as low as just 20 years during the neolithic period, then you can understand that infant mortality was a huge issue. People were now getting smarter and learning more about their surroundings, yet certain things they had to accept that they had no control over – and what could be more important to these people than fertility?

Fertility – this basically means 'productivity'. This could be the fertility of the land, the more fertile it is, then the more bountiful the crop yields are. Breeding with animals could mean some animals are more fertile and produce more offspring (or milk), so more productivity for the new year. With humans, the more children born will increase the chances of a stronger family or community and help counter the excessive premature losses. Also having no sickness or pension provisions, then having large families would also help safeguard the family in later years. Given all of this, this is something that people had no direct control over, so how best to counter this? Well, you can see throughout history, different cultures developed their own form of 'Gods' who, if appeased, would look more favourably upon their people. Yes, the wise men of the time sought the help of unknown and invisible forces that surround them and pray for their help. The people were very superstitious back then, but you can easily relate to our own modern religions and the practices that we still follow today. The Gods may be different, but the principles are still very much the same. If you have no control over something, then you pray to the Gods for help. So, to an early agricultural community, appeasing the Gods and ensuring a good harvest for the unknown coming year were vital. Fertility was therefore a very important feature to our ancestors, and we can see many Gods that were worshipped in relation to this. The influences of the Gods over the people would have been very powerful to these primitive people.

You can now imagine then that this whole topic is vast, and I cannot do it any justice here within this book, but you can sense the importance that fertility had many, many generations ago. This was a global ideology, with many different gods being worshipped in relation to fertility. If there is any doubt about how much this meant in England, then I would point to one fine mysterious example, the Giant Man of Cerne Abbas. This is a 55 metre, 180 ft. tall figure carved into the white chalk hills of Dorset. Up until recently, it has been very difficult to date such features, given that they were just shaped pits dug into the hillside and back filled with chalk. However, recent studies by the University of Gloucestershire and the National Trust have been able to date the sediments located at the base of the pits to be within a region dated between AD 700 to 1100 (using a complex technique of studying the stimulated luminescence of quartz crystals). Studies of snails (Cernuella virgata – or 'vineyard snail') inadvertently introduced to England by traders, also points to the giant dating to a period pre-1200.

Above: image of the Cerne Giant.

So, not a very recent creation then, yet this feature still survives today. It is said that if there was no upkeep to it, then the grass would have overgrown the figure within a 10-year period, which is believed to have happened at some point in it's past. This means that the local people cherished this chalk figure for generations, and effectively for over a thousand years. Incredible, yes? So, what is the symbolism. Well, it is plain to see to everyone, he is a nude male figure with a prominent erection and wielding a large wooden club in his right hand. Various ideas have been made about its purpose and origins, yet something that most antiquarians believe in is that it is linked to fertility. I don't think we can disagree with this, and rumour still holds today that people who sit upon him improve their fertility, and there have been numerous testimonies to this fact. I have no way of commenting upon this, but one thing is for sure in that the symbolism is evident and those ideas still abound into the present day.

The reason I mention the Cerne Abbas figure is the link that he still has with historical and present-day celebrations, as just like in the past, the May Day festivities are held above the giant's head. Morris men dance to welcome in the dawn on May Day, and in the past the local community would be dancing around a May Pole just above this figure, along with other May Day festivities. So, you see that at this particular location, there is a direct link here with the giant and also with the May Day celebrations and you will appreciate that the Pagan festivals around May were all to do with, that's right, 'fertility'.

Who does the giant represent then? Put it this way, nobody knows. That said, there have been many ideas and one of the favourites are that he represents the Roman hero and demigod – Hercules. This Roman hero was the equivalent to the Greek hero Heracles – who was the son of Zeus (Roman equivalent of Jupiter (God of the day and sky). Hercules was renowned for his strength, yet if we are to look at the date this was created – possibly 800-900 AD, then this does seem a bizarre choice, as clearly the giant represents 'fertility' rather than 'strength'. So, could this giant represent someone else? I think so…. So, let's explore that.

First things first, we have to accept that the figure is a 'giant' – hence his name – the Cerne Giant. That part cannot be overlooked. What other distinguishing features can be seen? Well, he is wielding an enormous wooden club with his right hand. Note, it is a club and not an axe/spear/sword etc. and the club is irregular shaped, not crafted for ease. So, can we find any other ancient drawings, pictures, sculptures etc. (other than Hercules) that features such examples? Well, yes, we can and lots of them. Due to copyright issues, I don't have any good examples to show you here, other than this coin, but I would ask that you just do an internet search for images of 'Medieval wild men holding clubs'. You can now appreciate that there are many examples. Correct? Now, here is the clincher… does the 'Wildman' feature in fertility and May Day celebrations?

Hold that thought.

Above: A coin from Germany of a Wildman holding a club. There are earlier representations from the Medieval period that will be shown later on.

One other thing that stands out is the name of the village itself, where the giant gets his name from – Cerne Abbas. Cerne could easily represent the Celtic God of the Forest – Cernunnos. And many people have made that connection. Cernunnos was a horned God of the forest associated with, you guessed it, fertility (animals and nature) and also for wealth – maybe pointing towards other ideas of 'productivity'. And 'Abbas' links in with St. Mary's Abbey, built in the late Saxon times (founded in AD 987), which is located at the base of the same hill. To counter this, the name is also attributed to Saint Augustine, who was the first Archbishop of Canterbury in AD 597 and was a Christian missionary sent by Pope Gregory the Great. Folk lore stories say that upon visiting the area, given that the local people were hostile to him, it is said that he remarked the Latin/Hebrew term 'Cerno deum' – which means 'I see God!' (Latin 'Cerno' – I see, and 'deum' Latin for God). Upon saying this, a spring emerged from the ground and the non-believers begged for forgiveness and then allowing Augustine to baptise them with the spring water. This sacred spring is still there today. I would also like to point out that Pope Gregory, in a letter in the year 601, to Abbot Mellitus (who had accompanied Augustine to England) that he should tell Augustine:

'What I have , upon mature deliberation, of the affair of the English, determined upon, viz, that the temples of the idols in those nations ought not to be destroyed; but let the idols that are in them be destroyed, let holy water be made and sprinkled in the said temples, let alters be erected and relics placed. For if those temples are well built, it is requisite that they be converted from the worship of devils to the service of the true God; that the nation seeing that their temples are not destroyed... may the more familiarly resort to the places to which they are accustomed.'

Well, this period of Augustine seems to point towards a date prior to the now believed construction of the giant, and for God , 'Cerno deum', to be seen in such a way is also not realistically credible – would you not agree? However, what we are aware of is that paganism was very much active at the cross over point with Christianity, as seen by Pope Gregory's letter of 601. It was a religious takeover, with the Pagan idols being destroyed, yet the temples just being converted to the new religion. Is it any wonder then that there should be stories surrounding Saint Augustine and the 'birth' of a sacred spring at this location, or should we say the birth of local religious propaganda – in the same way as we see the symbolism of the George and the Dragon story. The dragon possibly representing Paganism – and you will understand that at the time of the Saxons, early England (Wessex) flags were represented by a dragon, or Wyvern dragon to be precise. So, which of these ideas related to the Giant carry more credibility? Again, lets hold that thought for now.

Above: Flag of the Saxons: Wyvern Dragon.

The above flag, with a red background and gold wyvern (dragon) represented the historic region of Saxon Wessex. This flag was used as a banner carried into battle by the English until the 15th Century. It is considered to be England's first national flag and was, I understand, used by the English at the Battle of Hastings.

Cernunnos

Here we will take a closer look at the Pagan/Celtic God Cernunnos.

Cernunnos was a Celtic God of the forest that represents nature, fertility and animals. He is usually shown with deer antlers (or horns) and sitting cross-legged (like a Budda). He has a torc around his neck and is sometimes shown holding or surrounded by a bag of coins or grain. He has a beard, wild and bushy hair, the upper half of a man and the lower half of a goat or a stag. His actual name roughly translates as 'the horned one'. One interesting fact is that he is associated with male animals, particularly the stag and more so, a stag in rut. The autumn period of the rut is an incredible time to witness – where stags fight for dominance with their displaying, roaring and fighting abilities. A time where these majestic beasts would fight for favour over the herd. As a result, he is strongly associated with fertility rites. The winning stag would be the ruler over the forest! He was the true King of the forest!

Above: A nice representation of Cernunnos. Notice his connection with nature.

So, let's take a closer look at this remarkable Cernunnos. He was a very powerful God to these early pagan people. His distribution can be found in other parts of western Europe, but also in many parts of the British Isles. I think now we can see the logic behind the people of Star Carr, their beliefs didn't just appear out of nowhere.

So, the bag of coins or grain he has also symbolises wealth, fortune and productivity. The torc (from the Latin 'torquis') literally means 'twisted' as they are made from twisted metal. The torc itself marked nobility, upper social status, as well as power and strength, so you can already see that Cernunnos was regarded very highly by the Celtic traditions. Torcs were also awarded to brave warriors for distinguished acts in battles. Cernunnos is sometimes shown with a cornucopia. This comes from the Latin 'Cornu' meaning horn and 'Copia' meaning abundance. These were more commonly known as 'horns of plenty' as they were often shown with flowers and fruits spilling out of the opening. The horn of plenty appears in many different forms of mythology around the ancient world, but the meaning and symbolism still means the same – prosperity, wealth, abundance and productivity. You will often see these included at Harvest Festivals, symbolising the celebrations for the bounty received from the land at this time of year.

So, are we to believe that the Cerne Giant is a symbol of 'God' like Saint Augustine said he had witnessed, or Hercules – Roman demi God of strength? Or is he a representation of a Pagan God related to fertility? Given that the local traditions carry on celebrating May Day festivities here, all related to fertility, would also point to Cernunnos being that representation here. Agreed, the figure lacks horns, but was this always the case? There are other factors that might well have an influence here which we will look at later on, but certainly the figure could easily represent the Pagan 'Wildman' wielding a club, and this would link quite nicely with Cernunnos..

Now, let's carry on with this same thread.

Were there any other characters in history that appear to mirror Cernunnos? Well, yes. We can trace another God of the Wild to the times of ancient Greece. The God Pan, in Greek mythology was the god of the wild, shepherds, and rustic music (notably using the pan flute), he was also commonly associated with, you have probably guessed it, 'fertility', and also merriment/revelry. He was associated with sex and the season of Spring (May?). The literal meaning to the name Pan is 'everything' – as this meant everything from the natural world. The Greek God Pan was often shown as a human, but with the legs, horns and ears of a goat. He was believed to live in the mountains and forests of Greece. What more can be said about the Greek myth about Pan? Well, he enjoyed playing music and dancing with nymphs. Nymphs being yet another myth from Greece that are classed as lesser or inferior female divinities, usually beautiful maidens that inhabit trees (Meliae), mountains (Oreads), meadows, rivers or the sea (Oceanids). I will add that Oak tree nymphs were referred to as 'Dryads'.

Above: Greek coin from circa BC 310 – 303 representing Pan.

In Roman mythology, Pan is associated with 'Faunus' (the rustic God of the forest). Faunus was one of the oldest Roman deities. Faunus was celebrated and worshipped throughout the countryside given he was a bestower of fertility – be it flocks or crops!

Above: Representation of the Roman God Pan. Notice any similarities?

Pan/Faunus was also closely associated with the Roman God 'Silvanus' – who was a deity of the woods and uncultivated lands. He was a protector of the forests (Sylvestris deus), watching over the fields, protecting boundaries, cattle, flocks and also protector against wolves. Silvanus basically means 'of the woods'.

There is one more Roman God that needs to be mentioned here. Priapus. This Greek and Roman God was a god linked to fertility (animals and vegetables), gardens and the male genitalia. As seen in the included picture below, this God exhibited a large and permanent erection. We get the medical term 'priapism' from this god, which is defined by a prolonged erection lasting more than 3 to 4 hours. Below you can see an image of a small Roman statuette that I obtained related to this God. It may seem strange to us to see such images, but to the Romans, this formed part of their everyday life. Fertility was still a very important concept within their lives and gods like Priapus would have been worshipped, and small statuettes, like this example, would have been used as offerings to the god for their assistance. The power of faith, as you can appreciate, helps overcome difficult obstacles.

Above: Here you can see a small bronze figure of Priapus from Roman Times (AD 100 to 400). This statue most likely relates to a votive offering to this deity.

Was Priapus the only Greek/Roman God represented with a large phallus? Clearly not.

Pan was also seen represented with a huge phallus from time to time.

Faunus was often represented with an elongated phallus.

We also know that Priapus had an elongated phallus.

Cernunnos was sometimes represented with an erect phallus.

The overriding connection between all of these mythical Gods and deities were that they were associated with fertility. That connection cannot be overlooked. Most are also connected with the wild too.

The oldest known Pagan God, Inanna, was the Sumerian goddess of Love, fertility, procreation (but also the goddess of war). Worshipping Inanna can be traced back as far back as 3,400 BC. Her heritage appears to have followed through time being associated with the Assyrians (Ishtar), the Phoenicians (Astarte), the Greek (Aphrodite) and the Romans (Venus). Does it come as any great surprise that the earliest known spiritual concept worshipped in human history related to fertility?

Getting back to Cerne Abbas, was Hercules ever represented with a large phallus? Not according to my own research, and yet Hercules was not a deity related to fertility. So, I think we have our answer to the question who the Cerne Abbas Giant relates to, even if we don't understand specifically which deity this is, he was associated with Springtime celebrations and just like the traditions of re-chalking the giant, the May Day festivities carry on above the giant to this day. It forms part of an ongoing tradition. My own interpretation is that he represents the Wildman, who has close links with the forest Celtic God Cernunnos.

Now, Pan might be a Greek/Roman God associated with everything to do with nature and fertility, yet it will come as no great surprise that Satan is traditionally depicted as 'Pan'. Just do a web search for Pan and Devil. Quite the opposite of what this Pagan deity originally represented. Was that by pure chance? Of course not....

Let's ponder on that for a while....

So, the significance of the phallus on the Cerne Giant, given the cultural background, then I think it is safe to say that this relates to 'fertility' in some form or another. I don't think that argument can be disputed. Given this, we are now looking at Medieval and Pagan beliefs and celebrations related to fertility and especially May Day itself. My research into this area has taken me in all different directions, as you can tell, so we must appreciate that I can only give this a brief overview here.

Exactly how does this link in with Robin Hood? That's for the next chapter.... but just consider for a moment the fairy tale story of Peter Pan. Many people make the association between Peter Pan and Robin Hood. It is also true that James Mathew Barrie, the writer of Peter Pan (written in 1904) based Peter upon the mystical Greek character of Pan in remembrance of his older brother David, who died at the age of 14 from an ice-skating accident. The idea was that David will forever be young, just like Peter Pan – he will become immortal. Plus, Pan is associated with the fairy world, hence Tinker Bell. But in the past, I understood that Tinker Bell was only portrayed as 'lights' in shows, until, that is, Disney created her as a 'pixielike' figure in the animation film. Let's move on...

May Day Celebrations

Above: May Pole used at Highworth, Wiltshire, May Day 2024.

It was the Merry, Merry Month of May!

'The month of May has come, when every lusty heart beginneth to blossom, and to bring forth fruit'
– **Thomas Malory.**

'In the marvellous month of May, when all the buds were bursting, then in my heart did love arise'
– **Heinrich Heine.**

'May, more than any month of the year, wants us to feel most alive'
– Fennel Hudson.

'As full of spirit as the month of May, and as gorgeous as the sun in Midsummer'
– William Shakespeare.

I could continue with many more quotes about the month of May, but you will see from this small selection that May, above all months of the calendar year, is a time of great celebration. In modern times I feel we have lost a lot of the significance that this month offers us. To previous generations, it was a time of true celebration. The long, dark, cold winter months are all in the past and there was reason to enjoy the kinder, warmer months of summer. So, the first of May is significant in the medieval and pagan calendars. The whole countryside was bursting into life, flowers, blossoms and fresh growth everywhere you look. The weather becomes warmer, the daylight hours become longer, the whole mood of the people changes into a more positive way. It was no coincidence why we have the May Day Celebrations and just why it gets called the Merry, Merry Month of May!

How far back can we trace the Spring celebrations? Well, there are three significant ancient festivals that we need to look at:

Beltane

This was a Celtic festival held on the 1st of May within the British Isles. The festival was a celebration of fertility. Beltane, according to Celtic folklore, was married to Cernunnos, and she was the Goddess of Spring. Fires were created to recognise the halfway point of dark and light. Cattle were herded through avenues or around bonfires to cleanse them and rituals were performed for their protection before being taken to their summer pastures. All of the household fires would be put out and then relit with the embers of the Beltane bonfires. There would be feasting and merriment together with offerings to the mystic fairies and elves of the surrounding countryside (called the aos si, or similar). Houses and cattle would be decorated with Spring flowers – mainly yellow, possibly in symbolism with the sun or fire. Sometimes a May Bush would be created, typically a thorn bush (such as the Hawthorn/Whitethorn which would have been in blossom at this time) and cover them with flowers, ribbons and shells. Maidens would seek the early morning dew on May Day due to its magical qualities of enhancing beauty and youthfulness.

Above: Springtime whitethorn blossom starting to open.

Floralia

This was a roman celebration brought to the British Isles, which occurred between the latter part of April and the beginning of May. This whole celebration was related to the Roman god Flora, who was the goddess of flowers, spring and youth. Again, this was a celebration towards fertility and nature. She was very important to the Romans and celebrated in the Spring as she was believed to bring new energies to the world and as a consequence, breathe new life into people and encourage them to take action. Flora was understood to relate to a previous Greek mythology goddess – Chloris (goddess of flowers and Spring). The special flower associated with Flora was the rose – which symbolises both love and beauty.

It is worth noting that the Romans would honour Flora with festivals that includes games, feasts, hunting, theatrical entertainments, drinking and just merriments. It was a happy time to be alive!

May Day

Lastly, the May Day celebrations of the medieval period and those that we know of today. This has origins in both the above plus extra festivities that carry their own symbolism, but in short, it is another celebration towards fertility!

It is this period that we are most interested in as we know that Robin Hood was associated with the May Day festivities. It is well known about the 'Robin Hood Games' with the earliest reference to this being in 1426 from Exeter, which precedes the earliest ballad. It is uncertain how long these games were being held or just how widespread they were, but along with the ballads, this helps to confirm just how iconic Robin Hood was during the medieval period.

There are many different traditions that are scattered around the country, and it would not be possible to mention all of these. This book is aimed at Robin Hood's association with the May Day Celebrations. I think people can understand if they have attended a May Day festival and understand how happy the atmosphere is. This is true today as it was in the past, but one thing is crystal clear... this Day was far more important back then than it is today. Many of the old traditions are still very much alive today. Here are just a few that we know that have been handed down throughout the ages:

- Dancing around the May Pole
- Morris Dancers
- Selecting the May Day Queen
- Jack in the Green
- May Baskets – flowers given to people to cheer them up
- Bringing in the May – capture the morning dew, or collect flowers in the morning
- Lighting bonfires.

Some of these traditions may (pardon the pun) be old, but the traditions are still acted out every year doing the same thing... oral stories might change over time, but traditions remain traditional!

Above: Morris men dancing (Icknield Way Morris Men), Highworth, Wiltshire, May Day 2024. Notice the wooden sticks in use, there is a hidden link there (Cerne Giant & the Wildman?). Note: Icknield Way is claimed to be the oldest road in Britain and stretches from the Dorset Coast to Norfolk and it traces prehistoric pathways. Their emblem is a Wyvern Dragon too.

Robin Hood Games

These were held at a similar time as the May Day Celebrations yet were distinct and separate (or combined) and revolved around Robin Hood himself. They were very popular for a period of around 200 years in the 14th to 16th Centuries and would involve parades of people marching through the forests, countryside and around the towns and villages, with key characters dressed up accordingly leading the crowds. They would then return to festivities which would include games, such as archery, wrestling, ball games, racing etc. plus other rough and tumble activities. There would be feasting, drinking and all sorts of merry making. Robin would be the 'Lord of Misrule' and would be responsible for certain pranking on the day. Also, there would be many theatrical plays of the historical antics of Robin himself. This would possibly have been where the ballads initially developed from.

The first record of any form of Robin Hood play comes from 1426-27 from Exeter (so before the recorded ballads), and with the earliest extant text from a play coming from around half a century later from a 21-line fragment from East Anglia. This was known as 'Robyn Hod and the Shryff of Notyngham'. It was from these records from 1426/27 that there was a record of payments towards a Robin Hood play, however it does not confirm how widespread or how old these types of plays were known about, yet it certainly gives us a glimpse into this period. The Robin Hood celebrations were known to be quite raucous with some developing into riots and some were even designed in such a way to distract law enforcement to allow prison outbreaks. Oh yes, these were crazy days, but they were well attended and enjoyed by many.

Above: Antique solid bronze figure of Robin from the early 1900's. Robin has always been a popular figure.

Here is a reference I found from a book (written around 1860) about the games and just how popular they were at the time:

'This fact was attested by a Church of England Bishop of the 16th Century – the celebrated and venerable Latimer. In one of his pastoral visitations, he arrived in the evening at a small town near London, and gave notice that he should preach the next day, because it was a holyday. 'When I came there', says he, 'the Churche's door was fast locked; I tarried there half an hour and more, and at last the key was found, and one of the parishioners comes to me, and sayes 'Syr, this a busye day with us; we

cannot heare you; it is Robin Hood's day; the parish are gone abroad to gather for Robin Hood'.

Latimer had already put on his episcopal gown, but was obliged to take it off, and go forward on his way, leaving the place to the archers, dressed in green, who were enacting in a shady spot the parts of Robin Hood, Little John, and all the band.

Traces of the long-cherished recollection, which superseded in the breasts of the English people even the memory of the Norman Invasion, are at this day still existing.

From Ballads, Songs and Poems of Robin Hood – London, William Tegg, 1866.

You can see, just like in Piers Plowman, the draw of Robin Hood was far greater to the common people of this time than attending Church services. It was an important and joyous occasion in the annual calendar and this reference was from the 16th Century.

You can now see that Robin Hood was a celebrity of national significance.

Things to note: Robin was the Lord of Misrule, he played pranks and was responsible for the merry making.

One to ponder upon

Let's take another look at the characters of May Day and Robin Hood's Day. We have Robin Hood, naturally, we also have Maid Marion… but we also have Jack in the Green. Now Jack is a diminutive (to convey a sense of endearment) of the name John. Now could this relate to Little John? I cannot say one way or another, but certainly it appears that the dressing of a man 'in the green' could easily represent a disguise and given Robin Hood was often associated with Jack in the Green, it would seem appropriate that this character is linked more with Little John than Robin.

It is recognised that Marion and Friar Tuck were late comers to the tales of Robin Hood, and they were also associated with the May Games.

Above: Jack in the green – Highworth, Wiltshire, May Day 2024. Notice the crown of flowers.

Above: The author's wife posing with the Jack in the green troop, May Day, 2024.

The Wren and the Robin

Above: Decorative garden designs of the Wren and the Robin.

December 26th is well known for being Boxing Day, the day when the Church would open up its Alms/Collection boxes and distribute the contents to the poor. This is one of the Christian traditions. It is also the day that trades people and servants were given 'Christmas Boxes' by their masters or employers. But what happened on this day prior to this period and even, in some capacity, still happens to this very day? Well, within Celtic mythology, the wren (a native small brown bird), was regarded as the 'Holly King of Winter'. Yet tradition has it that this bird had a feud with another bird – the Robin. The Holly King, the wren, was driven away by the Robin on the Winter Solstice, because the Robin represented the 'Oak King of Summer'. These two birds would duel with each other for dominance over the seasons. The wren represented the winter, the brown vegetation dying off and the darkness whereas the Robin represented 'light', warmth, fertility and growth. This was a very unfair position being placed upon the wren, but we must remember that these people, hundreds of years ago, were very superstitious and did not fully understand how the seasons worked. They lived within the natural world, and they associated this with their beliefs. Indeed, within Norse mythology, the Robin was associated with the God Thor – the hammer wielding god associated with thunder and lightning, storms, trees and fertility. So, the Robin commanded a very powerful place in the mindset of our ancestors. Indeed, even today there is modern references that if you see a Robin then this means a passed loved one is nearby. Christian beliefs also build upon this by stating that the Robin's red breast was created from plucking the blooded thorns from Jesus's spiny crown when he was on the cross and staining his red breast. This gives the Robin a direct link to Christianity as it tried the relieve the suffering of Jesus at this time. These are all very symbolic and powerful features related to the Robin from all those years ago. Agreed?

But what about the little Wren? Unfortunately, he does not fare as well as the Robin. Wren Day (Irish: Lá an Dreoilín), or Hunt the Wren Day (Manx: Shelg yn Dreean) was a tradition held on Boxing Day. This related to Celtic traditions which still lives on in some rural parts of Ireland today, although luckily, not following the original concept. Basically, in olden days, mainly groups of boys and men would seek out and kill a wren and parade it around the village hanging it from a pole. The 'Wren Boys' would then ask for money from people in their homes otherwise they would bury the wren at their doorstep and bad fortune would follow on that homeowner for the next year. The modern 'Wren Day' is celebrated by bands of people descending upon people's homes whilst singing and dancing and bringing good fortune and merriment to the owners, and then requesting a donation for their time.

However, it is understood that the original reason behind this day was due to the belief that the battle between the Wren and Robin was always a concern and that by killing wrens would help weaken their power and control over the winter months and would help usher in an early spring and summer, strengthening the power of the Robin.

It is ironic that despite the wren being one of the most common breeding birds in the UK, due to its tiny size, their populations suffer large declines during severe and prolonged winter months. So not quite the Holly Winter God our ancestors would have you believe. But what we can tell from these previous traditions is that the Robin was very important back then...... very important. It is also noteworthy to understand that the Christian Church tried to include the symbolism of the Robin.

Does any of this spill over into our modern-day traditions? Well, yes, it does. I think it is safe to say that this is partly why you see Robins represented upon Christmas Cards to this very day. Is this related to the Christian or Pagan narrative? Or both? You decide.

You have to remember the manner in which our ancestors' minds worked.... everything, or at least just about everything, related to or revolved around the natural world. Pagan people would study nature and believed the natural world to be sacred. They witnessed the natural cycles of fertility, birth, growth, ageing, death and they would place spiritual meanings on this. They would have seen that our own development fitted in with this natural cycle of life. Humans, plants, trees, animals, even rocks were interconnected. This is why a lot of the early gods were directly associated with the natural world – indeed, the Romans had several main Gods:

Jupiter:	God of the sky and thunder.
Juno:	Goddess of women, marriage and childbirth.
Vesta:	Goddess of hearth, home and family.
Ceres:	Goddess of agriculture, grain crops, fertility and motherly relationships.
Mercury:	God of commerce, travellers, messengers and trickery. He also guided people to the underworld.
Mars:	Originally a God associated with agriculture, later to also become the God of war.
Apollo:	The God of the sun and of light. But he also was the god of poetry, music, knowledge, prophecy, order, plagues, beauty, agriculture and also – archery!

Diana:	Goddess of wild animals and hunting.
Vulcan:	The God of fire and the forge and metal working.
Neptune (Greek: Poseidon):	God of the Sea and water, earthquakes and horses.
Minerva:	Goddess of wisdom, art, schools, justice, war and commerce.
Venus:	Goddess of love and beauty. Associated with the Greek Goddess Aphrodite, which was still worshipped during the Roman period.

Although this is a list of the main Roman Gods, there were many. This was partly due to the expansion of the Roman Empire incorporating different civilizations and then adopting or incorporating elements of these over time. You can already see an overlap between some Greek and Roman Gods, and this is what happened throughout this period. It all becomes very complex, but you can see the relevance that these Gods and Goddess's have with the daily lives of people. The natural, and human, world was controlled by these **invisible** spiritual beings and in order to appease them, they were worshipped, celebrated and offerings, even sacrifices, being made in their honour. This was their understanding and beliefs. You can appreciate why given that there were no technical understandings why the world worked the way it did. It was their way of making sense of a complex world and why things happened the way they did. Modern day religion is no different in that people pray for guidance from their own Gods. I think we can now buy into this bygone ethos.

Now, there are a couple of extra Gods here that I want to mention that will have a bearing upon later chapters.

Roman Goddess Flora

She was the Goddess of Flowers, the coming of Spring and the fertility of the land. This Goddess was known of before the establishment of the Roman Republic (509 BCE to 27 BCE), and its believed origins can be traced back to Greek mythology and the Goddess Chloris (Khloris), who was associated with spring, flowers and new growth. We can see the relevance of Flora in our modern-day world, as she was associated with Roses – which symbolises love and beauty. So, when you give (or receive) roses then this is the reason behind this very old tradition – it's in reference to the Goddess of Love – Flora. I'm sure this is why the flower delivery company – Interflora, got its name.

Cupid – derived from the Greek God Eros (meaning erotic):

Above: Artistic representation of Eros and Psyche.

Cupid was the Roman God of desire, erotic love, passion, attraction and affection. He was also known as Amor ('love'). He is regarded as being the son of the union between Venus (goddess of love) and possibly Mars (God of war). He was portrayed as a winged young child holding a bow and arrow, which is different to Eros, who was more like an athletic youth/young man. Cupid had feathery wings as love can be flighty and lovers can change their minds quickly, and he was a boy as love can be irrational and hold no logic. Cupid might also hold a fire torch as well as the bow and arrows – because 'love wounds' and can 'inflame the heart' with a burning desire. Cupid might also be blindfolded or shown to be blind – because 'love can be blind'. Cupid gets a mention in Shakespeare's Midsummer Night's Dream, which I think helps add more context to the role Cupid has.

Love looks not with the eyes, but with the mind
And therefore is winged Cupid painted blind.
Nor hath love's mind of any judgement taste;
Wings and no eyes figure unheedy haste.
And therefore is love said to be a child
Because in choice he is so oft beguiled.

In some ancient Roman art, Cupid was surrounded by animals, fruits, or a bearing of the seasons. He also carries two types of arrows – one sharp with a golden point – which helps people fall in love, and then an arrow with a blunt tip made of lead, which gives a person aversion to desire and a will to flee or even a change in destiny.

The Greek God Eros was said to have made a lot of people happy by his interventions of love, then after many years of being alone he eventually fell in love himself and eventually married a beautiful human woman, a princess called Psyche. The Greek translation for her name was 'Soul', and she was to eventually be granted the gift of immortality. Her beauty was renowned to rival Aphrodite (Goddess of Love and associated with the Roman God Venus). Within the myths, Psyche was given multiple trials by Aphrodite to be with her love, Eros. A lot of this is recorded within the stories of the Golden Ass, a second century AD novel (consisting of 11 books) written in Latin by a Roman Philosopher - Apuleius. Most of the books revolve around a man called Lucius, who dabbles in magic to turn himself into a bird, but it goes horribly wrong, and he turns himself into a donkey. In order to resolve the situation, he goes on travels and is eventually helped by the Goddess Isis. However, on the way he hears many stories, including tales about Socrates, the activities of a group of bandits, and more importantly, he hears about the love story of Psyche and Eros or Cupid in this context.

In short summary, Psyche, despite her beauty, could not find her suitor so her father, a King, sort guidance from an Oracle, who only gave bad news. The King followed the Oracles orders nonetheless, and made his daughter stand upon the tallest rock spire and await her fate – to face a beast, yet it never came. Instead, **an invisible Eros** was watching her. The mighty west wind blew her away from the rock spire where she fell into a deep sleep. When she awoke, she was in a palace full of riches. An **invisible** voice told her to make herself at home and that everything there belongs to her now. She took a bath and ate well at the same time as an **invisible** lyre played wonderful music for her. It then dawned on her that this **invisible person** was her potential new husband. He only came at nighttime and always **remained invisible**, not wanting Psyche to understand who he really was. He wanted her to regard him as an equal rather than reveal his true identity. This worked fine up until Psyche had her family visit, who naturally wanted to know who her believed husband really was. Psyche did not say anything at first, but later explained the situation. Her jealous sisters told her to sneak into his room when he was asleep and kill him. Reluctantly she was persuaded to do this and one night she sneaked into Eros's room with an oil lamp and a dagger. Holding the oil lamp over Eros she instantly saw that her husband was a God, and the shock made her spill some of the hot oil on Eros's shoulder.

She realised her error and immediately dropped her plan of murdering her husband. The drop of oil awoke Eros and knowing he had been betrayed, he took flight. In an instant, the palace disappeared, and Psyche found herself stranded near to her family home.

The injury from the oil was attended to by Eros's mother – Aphrodite, where she learned about the union of her son with Psyche. Later, Psyche sought forgiveness from an angry Aphrodite, who then had her whipped and tortured. Afterwards she was given some impossible trials. First was a barrel full of grains, barley, beans, poppy seeds and wheat, all mixed together and she was told to sort these by the end of the day. An ant watched Psyche's pain and got the whole of its nest to sort the grains. Once completed, this angered Aphrodite even more.

The next trial was for Psyche to shear the golden fleece of a renowned dangerous pack of rams. Rather than face this trial, she decided to drown herself in a nearby river, only for the River God, Potamoi, telling her not to pollute his waters. He then gave her advice on how to approach the rams and that was, when the weather got cooler, as they were less likely to attack her. This she did and achieved shearing the golden fleeces from the rams. This was not enough for Aphrodite.

The third task given to her was to obtain a crystal cup of water from the black waters of the River Styx. Upon arrival towards the river, Psyche was filled with despair as she would have to climb a dangerous cliff in order to reach the river. Luckily, Zeus was watching and took pity on her and used an eagle to fetch the water for her. This was still not enough for Aphrodite.

Psyche's final task was yet again another impossible task. She was told to take a golden box to the underworld and obtain some of the beauty possessed by the Goddess of Spring and the Queen of the Underworld, Persephone. How? The task was impossible, so faced with this she once again decided she would take her own life. She walked up to the top of a tall tower in readiness to throw herself over the walls. However, the tower spoke to her and told her to travel to the boundary with Sparta where a pathway to the underworld will be revealed to her. Upon reaching there she was shocked to see Persephone waiting for her and she happily filled the golden box with her beauty. Psyche then returned having fulfilled her task, but her curiosity got the better of her and she opened the box to gaze inside... upon which she found the box housed a dark cloud that immediately sent her into a deep sleep.

Psyche was not having much luck despite completing her impossible tasks.... but that was about to change. Eros had now recovered from his injuries and went looking for his love. When he found her, he awoke her with one of his arrows. He took the golden box to his mother and then went and pleaded with Zeus in order to help protect Psyche. This he granted and in exchange for helping the loving pair, he wanted Eros to help him when he desired the attentions of any future maiden. Eros agreed and then all the Gods were called upon to witness Zeus's word. He called upon Aphrodite to never harm Psyche again, and then he handed Psyche a cup with ambrosia, the drink of the Gods that granted immortality. This was followed by a great celebration as Eros and Psyche were married. The pair later had a child, Hedone, who became the Goddess of pleasure.

Above: A small Roman statuette (2nd/3rd Century) of Eros with him reaching into his arrow bag, together with his wings. Not invisible here.

Roman God Silvanus

The name literally means in Latin 'of the woods'. Sylvestris deus – was a protector or guardian deity of the woods and uncultivated lands. He took great pleasure with all the trees going wild. Silva is the Latin name for forest/wood.

Within Britain there have been references associated with the Roman God of the Forest and that of the earlier local Celtic God of the Forests – Callirus. Several wall plaques were found in Camulodunum (modern day Colchester) within a Romano-Celtic temple dedicated to 'Silvanus Callirius'. How was this represented? Well, as a stag. Stags were iconic animals of the forest, their antlers looked like branches growing from their heads. They represented strength, speed, wariness, vitality and above all - fertility. A feature that would not have gone un-noticed by the people of the time, as they watched stags fighting each other during the autumnal rut.

Roman God - Sol

Sol was the Roman Sun God. There are differing opinions if there were two Sun Gods or this was one and the same, but just changed its influence from the early to the later Roman period. What is for sure is that by the later times, prior to adopting Christianity, Sol was very important, and 'Sol Invictus' (the 'unconquered sun') was a major winter festival. The significance of this was discussed in my previous book, but we will take another look at this later. As a side note, the Goddess Luna, the moon Goddess, is personified as the corresponding female counterpart to Sol.

Above: Constantine I (The Great) Bronze Follis coin – circa: 307 to 337 AD – depicting Sol – the Pagan Sun God
(prior to the change in the Roman religion).

You can appreciate that the Romans worshipped many gods, but what has this got to do with Robin Hood? Bear with me. This is a journey that we are on, and you need to take on board a wider background to the influences that would have a knock-on effect to later times. You will notice that some of the things mentioned above even have a direct link to our own modern-day world. The tradition of giving roses for example. Roman words, beliefs, traditions and influences still live on, and this would have been more apparent during the Middle Ages where in the early part, documents and manuscripts were mostly recorded in Latin.

Out of all the above, I want to underline the significance of Eros. I believe he played a pivotal role in the development of the stories surrounding our Robin Hood.

Let's start to bring some of this together as we try to track down the real person behind the Robin Hood legend.

Back to linking Robin

We know that in 1377, within the first reference to Robin Hood in Piers Plowman, he was recognised as a very famous character, indeed, to the point that a priest knew the verses of Robin Hood better than he knew of the Lords Prayer. How can that be? No doubt this is an exaggeration, but one thing is clear and that is that Robin held a widespread reputation at this time. So, if he was that well known, why isn't there any clear references recorded in history – such as within the Saxon Chronicles? It doesn't really make any sense. People have searched and searched, yet the person remains a mystery. Or does he?

We are all familiar with the proverb saying that history is recorded by the victors and that their version will be the one that survives through the ages, including all their biases that accompany it. We see that recorded within the Bayeux tapestry in captivating visual form. That has all been reinforced upon us all through the ages. We accept this.

That said, what can we say about the defeated? What is their story? Will the legacy of the native Anglo-Saxons all be forgotten about and wiped out from the history books? There will be no tapestry telling their story. So, how would you tell your story in a way that will appeal to all the demoralised and defeated people of England, one that can be openly played out and install a sense of hope. Yes, <u>hope!</u> You will appreciate that there were many revolts and disagreements with the new King of England – William the Conqueror. His desire to rule over a united country still hung in the balance. His win at Hastings was only the start of his struggles. Only some of the English Earls and Barons pledged their allegiance to him initially. So, it is true that he didn't have an easy time winning over the people of England. As a result, he was brutal to all that stood in his path. Absolutely brutal. And that aspect is nicely played out in all the Robin Hood films – correct?

You can now imagine that the people of England needed a hero, someone that symbolised their struggle against oppression. Someone that shared their Anglo-Saxon way of life. Someone they can believe in, someone strong, brave, smart and carry the weight and hopes of a conquered nation on their shoulders. The time was ripe for a hero. Did one exist? Did one of them stand out above all others who could represent these hopes? A person with legend qualities, the likes of King Arthur. Someone who would stand up to these new Norman usurpers.

There was only one big problem. If you are the defeated and suppressed in such brutal ways, as the Anglo-Saxons were at this time, then how would any form of hope be installed within the population. To talk openly of resistance would be stamped upon very quickly and the punishments would have been severe. The people needed someone to believe in, but in such a way that does not arouse suspicion or be deemed supporting resistance. Did such a person exist? In answer to this – Yes! That person we know as Robin Hood.

This character from the Middle Ages has forged an everlasting set of tales into our mental psyche. He is a blast from Anglo-Saxon England times and even today we marvel at this legend in many ways. Every generation have their own films about him and they are portrayed in ways that appeal to the modern audience. It is incredible to think that the ones considered as the defeated are the ones that are celebrated into modern times – nearly a thousand years later! What can be said about the Conqueror? I have yet to see any film where he is portrayed in a good way, let alone a film itself. So, through the eyes of Robin Hood, we are seeing the story of the defeated. Yes, a hero of his time, yet one who's country had been conquered. Is it any wonder why we see more references to Robin Hood through the ages than we do for William. He appealed to most of the population of the time and that has been handed down through the ages in one way or another. His stories have all changed as every generation rewrites or adds a new version, character or plot. Like all good legends told by word of mouth, the starting point is very different to the end.

But where was that starting point? Lots of scholars believe his origins trace back to the time of Prince John and King Richard and that is based upon the recorded ballads of the 1450's onwards. The first written record being Robin Hood and the Monk. King Richard became King in 1189 and died in 1199 and he rarely stayed in England. So, the earliest recoded ballad is written over 250 years later, giving plenty of time for the oral stories to be altered.

Again, why would such a larger-than-life character appeal to so many people, yet there are no written records of who that person really was? When do you feel this character would appear as a symbol of hope for the Anglo-Saxon people? Thinking about it, would that be hundreds of years after the biggest event that shook the status quo of Anglo-Saxon England? Or maybe, just maybe, it was at that same time period when the country and its people were torn apart and thrown into a state of turmoil - **chaos**? Would that person representing 'hope' be a person that the Normans would be happy to acknowledge or even put up with? Of course not.

So, let's take another look at the name Robin Hood. Like I mentioned earlier, when I asked you to google a 'hooded person' – you will instantly see what I am getting at here. As we know, in the early Middle Ages, surnames were first adopted in such a way that helped add extra relevance to the person in question. Surnames could describe the type of trade someone had, the location they came from, their hereditary links such as 'son of', or, in the consideration we are looking at here, an attribute – be it to their character or other quality. When we see a picture of a hooded person, we instantly recognise a person whose face is hidden. A hood did just that, and this is where we get the expression of hoodwinked – 'to deceive by false appearance' or, in essence, to 'bluff'. Is this what our hero was? Someone created to deceive. Was this hooded man an alias? After all, we are aware from the tales that Robin was a master of disguise. Is this a thousand-year-old disguise that has kept us all guessing through the ages? Is it a legend that will never be solved? To date, there is no clear answer to the true identity of Robin Hood, indeed the consensus is that he is a fabrication of many folklore stories rolled into one from a bygone era.

That said, I believe the true origins behind the legend are in fact real, and also based upon someone truly fitting of the hero that we see represented today. Yes, he was real, very real... yet was his name really Robin Hood? Like I said earlier, if the Normans really knew, then many heads would roll in suppressing any sense of resistance from the populace. So, his name is most likely an alias, hence why we have the 'hooded' character, both by name and by nature! Have all those attempts at trying to find a Robin Hood in the history books been wasted? Well, no, not really... you need to test the obvious before looking at the alternatives and tracing a real-life living character from this time period by the name of Robin Hood has not borne any fruit. There are a number of possibles, yet none tick all the right boxes. I won't go into any detail regarding these candidates, but you can read a number of books regarding these alternatives. And for those who have studied the origins of Robin Hood will fully understand what I am getting at here.

Let's start looking at some of the things that we understand about Robin and use this as our base lines for searching for the man behind the legend.

Robin Hood

An oral tradition, by definition, leaves no written records!

The above statement is very telling.

So, what do we know about him, or believe to know about him, let's remind ourselves:

- He was an Anglo Saxon (not Norman or Anglo-Norman).
- Either a yeoman or a nobleman, depending upon the references made.
- He was an outlaw.
- He hid in the forest to evade capture – possibly Sherwood Forest.
- The forest was enchanted/haunted.
- He took from the rich and the corrupt church, including, we understand, the Sheriff of Nottingham (or equivalent?).
- He gave to the poor.
- He used bow and arrows.
- He was dressed in green.
- He had his lands taken from him by the Normans.
- He pleaded fidelity/loyalty to the King.
- He had met the King.
- He later went into the service of the King.
- He and his men, go on quests.
- He had a band of 'Merry' men.
- He represented defiance to oppression.
- He was a man of disguise.
- He was a real-life folk hero to the common people, and at a later date, to the upper classes.
- His original stories would have been told orally and handed down through the ages.
- He was believed to have come from Lockersley/Lockley/Loxley.
- His earliest stories come from ballads, initially from around 1450.
- He is first mentioned in 1377 in Piers Plowman.
- There are no official documents that confirm his true identity.
- The person behind the legend remains unknown.
- He is associated with the May Day celebrations.

May?

When we start thinking about May, there is every reason as to why it became a time of real celebration. It was a celebration of the summer months ahead, a new beginning for the growing season. The countryside was alive and starting to flourish. Everywhere May flowers and blossom would be flowering and blooming – it was an omen of the trials of the previous winter months were truly over with. It was a time of new beginnings and good times ahead. A time of 'hope'. It was also a merry time! Indeed, the merry, merry month of May!

As a supplementary note, it is worth nothing that in 1620 the sailing ship 'Mayflower' transported the Pilgrim Fathers to the New World – landing off Cape Cod, Massachusetts on November the 21st. The site was originally surveyed and named earlier by a Captain John Smith. Due to their religious beliefs differing from the Church of England, they decided that America offered them the promised land! They succeeded and established the Plymouth Colony – the founding permanent English colony in New England, and the third overall in America. They arrived just as winter was approaching and around half of the settlers did not make it through to the following summer. Possibly more would have died if they did not gain the assistance of the local indigenous people. Those that survived the winter (53 of them) celebrated the first year's harvest the following autumn, along with the local native Americans. This marks the importance of the 'Thanksgiving' celebrations held in the American annual calendar.

Now, can you imagine a better name for the Puritans travelling to the New World in 1620 could name their ship? Was it pure coincidence or was there thought put into this? Given that two ships were meant to sail, but due to issues with 'Speedwell' only the Mayflower departed. Was this just a coincidence or was it fate? I have not researched into this, but the 'Mayflower' is an appropriate name for a trip to the New World, a name that will carry the same 'hope' of new beginnings and favourable times. The symbolism here is striking, and it appears that the magic of the flowers of May brought good luck to these pioneering travellers.

So why would Robin Hood be a person associated with the May Day celebrations? He was an outlaw after all. We will take a closer look at that later.

Loxley or Lockersley?

The Sloane manuscripts in the British Museum (handwritten prose believed to have been composed towards the end of the 16th. Century and gives the earliest stories about Robin Hood's background) have an account of Robin's life which states that he was born around 1160 associated with a place called **Lockersley.**

It is understood that Loxley or Lockersley, Lockley, or Locksleaigh are fictional names for where Robin came from.... but I believe it maybe an accurate synonym to the truth. Instead of looking for a place called Loxley/Lockersley etc. which does not exist (in the context that we are looking for, linked to Nottingham), so let's take a closer look at the possible links to the name and break it down. 'Lock' comes from an old English word 'Loc' meaning 'bolt' or enclosure, a door fastening... and 'Leah' comes from the old English 'Leah' which means 'clearing in a forest'. Interesting that in the English language we have the word 'bolt-hole' which also means 'a place where a person can escape or hide'.

So, what I am suggesting is that this could be some type of artistic licence used here. Or do we have yet another reference to a forest hideaway for Robin Hood. Why Lockersley? Is that just too much of a coincidence or do you think there is a strong link to the truth here. When studying this subject, I feel there is no such thing as a coincidence. Remember that when looking at early English words, there were variations due to the way in which they were written (due to no standardisation), the different languages used and the people who wrote them (their spelling). So, given the old English words used here, was this purely a translation issue based upon oral traditions?

If this is the case, then isn't this interesting how a previous writer could have transferred a possible old English phrase into an actual settlement name that is then associated with Robin Hood. It is also helpful in revealing how a story could be distorted over time when different people have added their own interpretations to the previous held storyline. Naturally, I cannot say with any certainty that this is the case, but this is the first time I believe this point has been raised and it can only help towards the discussions – but I think this is a very valid possibility here.

Also, when it states that Robin was born here.... Does that mean physically 'born', or where the legend was born?

Interestingly, this is also where the surnames Lee, Lea and Leigh would partly have originated from too.

There is a Loxley in South Yorkshire and also a Loxley in Warwickshire too. 'Lox', as far as I can see, historically relates to Salmon. There is, however, a 'Lockley Wood', near Hinstock in Shropshire.

Hold that thought!

Initial Connections

Now we are starting to think outside of the box, our attention now turns in a different direction

I would here like to briefly describe a story written as a Play from a book called 'Merrie England' a book of Plays – with one particular short story called 'Jack-In-The-Green' written by Vilolet M. Methley. This story dates to around the 1920/30's, unfortunately the book does not include a publication date. It follows the storylines of Prince Charles (later to become King Charles II). This is a dramatisation, given that the real Prince Charles sought refuge in 1651 by concealing himself in an oak tree near Boscobel House, south-east Shropshire, in order to evade Parliamentarian forces. It was also interesting to note that Boscobel House is just a mile south of Watling Street – one of the main routes that Robin Hood would have been associated with. Understandably, this is just a story, and we have no idea behind the reasons it was written, but I think it perfectly confirms just how the early references to Robin Hood can be morphed into a more modern-day version, although set in the 17th. Century.

The setting is a village May Day celebration, with children dancing around the Maypole and Morris Dancers doing their moves. It is noted that the Morris Dancers are referred to as Sweeps – i.e. chimney sweeps – all with blackened faces due to soot. May Day is a 'great festival of all sweeps' (please take notice of the link here). Prince Charles turns up dressed in rags, but he is later recognised. This said, the most important character from the story is:

> 'And here is our Leader, our Jack you will see!
> All dressed in green branches, as fine as he can be!'
> 'Here come to the Maying, we've come to the fun!'

'An' here be I, Jack-In-The-Green, that was once Melvas, King of Somerset, who dressed in green boughs and lay await to steal Queen Jennifer, King Arthur's Queen, as she went a-maying. An' so I do be condemned to lie always hid in green; but I come, too, to make merry with you all this May-day.'

As the Prince has been recognised, he speaks out declaring that it is he and that there is a reward of 100 guineas on his head, and if anyone wants to take that reward then this was their chance! All people present shout out that they are all Royalists, and that the Prince can trust them. A young boy states that he had overheard officials talking about the prince heading in this direction, so he should hide.

Jack says that there is only one place to hide and that is 'here, in the Green'. But first he should blacken his face to conceal his identity and blend in with the other chimney sweeps.

The prince thanks Jack, but Jack responds:

> 'I need no thanks, your Highness. A King's Man I've always been and always will be, God bless him! Now, quick, inside the Green'

The May Day festival continues.

Later the official turns up who has a very dim view of the local people with their May Day celebrations. He proceeds to stop the festival calling them rogues and vagabonds.

Jack responds: 'Rouges, indeed! Vagabonds, indeed! I'll have you know that we are members of the Worshipful Society of Master-Sweeps – honest workingmen, who do but take their holyday a' May-day, like all good sweeps. These are our Lord and Lady; this is our Jack-In-The-Green, and these four climbing boys'.

The officials respond by asking who they were to talk 'so big?'

Jack himself responds: 'Why, see you not my garments? Robin Hood, I am, come from the greenwood'.

The official goes around searching for the prince. Approaching Jack, the official asks Jack to remove his black soot from his face so he can readily see him. Jack refuses and the official then notices a blackened face within the Jack-in-the-green structure and demands that they and all the sweeps, all clean their faces. Jack refuses, so the official says that Jack will be put in the village stocks for his insolent behaviour. A touch of humour then proceeds with Jack going to the stocks and pretending that he doesn't understand how they work and puts his arm into the feet holes. The Official calls him an idiot and then shows him how it works by sitting in the stocks, at which point Jack closes the stocks and locks the official in it. The official is angry and demands that he is released, but Jack's response is:

'Nay, sir, speak not ill of your own medicine! It will cool your proud spirit to sit there a while.' (laughing).

They all then sing a May Day song, and the prince is saved from capture.

Note: Climbing Boys is reference to the young boys used for cleaning chimneys (given that they were small enough to climb up these dirty enclosed spaces) and they are remembered and honoured in England during May. May Day itself was also a holiday for the 'climbing boys' and they would joyfully dance through the streets. This would be due to the fact that it was now summer, so people would not be heating their homes with fires during the following summer months.

Although this is still a new chapter in the stories related to Robin Hood, it was the first reference that I had found linking Robin Hood with the May Day Celebrations and the Green Man. When I wrote my first book, I had made reference to Robin Hood having some associations with the green man, more so than its historical legends, and sure enough, my thinking was starting to take on some relevance here. This was my starting point in digging deeper into the May Day Celebrations.

The Green Man of England

Above: Iconic Green Man medieval church sculpture
with oak leaves and acorns.

I'm sure most people will have heard about the Green Man. Lots of people might have had a pint in a Green Man pub that are dotted around the countryside of the British Isles (and beyond). I would be one of them. Indeed, there is a Green Man pub located just outside the neighbouring village that I grew up in, a village called Abthorpe, in South Northamptonshire. The neighbouring village in question will be one that many people have heard about around the world, especially if they are Formula One enthusiasts, as the village I am talking about is Silverstone. Is it by chance that the pub is called the Green Man? I don't know, as I have not traced its origins, but I believe that this probably dates back quite a few years (as most do). Afterall, the village of Silverstone gets its name from the Latin 'Silva' meaning woodland and 'tun' or 'ton' meaning 'town' or settlement in Medieval times. In late Medieval times the village was called 'Silverton' as referenced here with a map from John Speed, from around 1611. So, this would have linked into the idea that the village was located within a forest and that is understandable, as there are still forests located outside Silverstone today - Hazelborough Wood and Bucknell Wood, and this is where I went exploring many times during my youth. So, is it any wonder why there is a Green Man pub just outside Silverstone, and also being adjacent to Hazelborough Wood? Not really. When you start looking at history, there is usually an explanation behind places and names.

Above: From a map of Northamptonshire by John Speed (c. 1611) with a close up of 'Silverton' (modern day Silverstone). You can see 'Wood Forest' next to it. Just above it is the village that the author grew up in – listed here as A'throrp (modern day Abthorpe).

Above: It was also interesting to note during my research that Abthorpe (Althrop) was also enclosed by the same woodland in 1695 – From a later Robert Mordon map.

The green man, as portrayed upon Churches and Pub signs represent a face hidden behind vegetation. The images are long held to represent the spirit of nature together with 'fertility'. They are often shown represented with fruits or berries and more often with acorns. They are very often found on Churches that date back to the Norman times. They first started appearing in the early 12th Century in England, although their symbolism can be traced back to earlier times and cultures. The fact that they can be first traced back to the EARLY 12th Century in England is striking and may have influence upon later chapters.

The Oak Man.

Above: The Akeman Inn, Buckinghamshire.

The green man maybe familiar to everyone, but it doesn't end there. Recently, whilst on a trip to Aylesbury, I was driving along the A 41 through a place called Kings Wood in Buckinghamshire and then, just on the outskirts, there was a pub called the Akeman Inn – together with the green man looking design. So, I had to stop and take a picture and only upon getting home and researching it's meaning that it all became clear. The word 'Ake' comes from the Anglo-Saxon name for 'Oak'- and then 'Man'. How interesting was this and this was the first time that I had come across this. Yet again, the coincidence of this green man type pub being found on the outskirts of a place called 'Kings Wood' is no coincidence. I'm sure this name is how we also got the name of acorns. Makes sense, doesn't it? The significance of the Oak will become apparent later on.

So, who does the Green Man/ Oak Man actually represent? Well throughout the ages the idea behind the Green Man has changed. If we start looking back at folklore, then we will see that there are many takes on the spirits of the woods. Pan, Silvanus, Cernunnos, Fairies, Goblins, Elves, Hobgoblins,Woodwusa, Wildmen, Green man, in fact the list can go on for ages, and when including stories from different countries or cultures, then this list could be endless. In North America we get the modern variation to this and that is Sasquatch or Bigfoot! Yes, Bigfoot.

How can we be talking about Bigfoot, Wildman and Robin Hood in the same document? Well, that is exactly why you need to read to the end of the book. So, without any further delay, let's look at some of the historical stories and then surprisingly, some more modern ones about the Wildman.

Above: The Akeman Inn, Buckinghamshire.

Wildman stories from our past

What other stories do we know from the past that has links to the Wildman? Well, this will come as a surprise to you. Let's start with Robinson Crusoe – a novel written by Daniel Defoe, published in 1719 and relates to a castaway due to a shipwreck in the Caribbean. Robinson lived a secluded life for 28 years and 2 months and 19 days on a deserted island, with his only companion being a native which he called Friday who he had rescued from some cannibals. Friday being the day that he was rescued. OK, but where did that inspiration come from? Well, it can be traced back to a real-life person called Alexander Selkirk (1676 – 1721) who was a Scottish privateer (legalised piracy) and Royal Navy officer. So, Selkirk, unlike Crusoe, was basically a pirate, and his voyages would see him raiding upon Spanish ships and coastal cities of South America. Selkirk was left on an uninhabited island in the South Pacific (not the Caribbean) for four years and four months through choice, not due to a shipwreck. This was that he feared that the ship he was travelling on (Clinque Ports) was doomed and preferred his chances to be left on an island – the Mas a Tierra (now known as Robinson

Crusoe Island), 416 miles off the coast of Chilie. During his stay, he evaded capture from two Spanish ships, then, later on, to be rescued by another British privateer ship. The ship's crew were greeted by a man covered in goat skins and looking like a 'wildman' himself. Luckily one of the men on the ship, William Dampier, vouched for Selkirk, having worked alongside him in the past. It was good fortune for Selkirk as the Clinque Ports had sunk off the coast of Puru with all of its crew, bar the captain and 7 other men, all being perished. The fate of the survivors was probably worse, being left to rot in a Peruvian prison.

Now for the interesting part. One year into his island isolation, due to the aggressive nature of the sea lions at the foreshore, he moved inland where he encountered a large wild hairy human, it was something that he related to from what his father had told him about the Big Grey Man from Scotland when he was a child, however he described it best as a woodwose. His account explains how he attempted to communicate with the being over a period of time, yet a violent dispute over some goat meat, which ended by Selkerk using gunpowder, and this scared it away. He never saw it again and regretted his actions.

His experiences were then adapted by Defore with Robinson Crusoe, however Defoe transformed the Wildman character from his account into the fictionalised figure of Friday, a native that Crusoe rescued.

Sir Gwain and the Green Knight.

This is one of the best Arthurian Stories from the past, which dates back to at least the late 14th Century. It is a chivalric romance story about a knight, who was not yet a knight of Arthur's Round Table, yet involved a challenge with a mysterious Green Knight.

It was at a Christmas period celebration at Camelot when King Arthur requests any fascinating stories or adventures anyone could tell, when at that moment a gigantic green figure burst into the hall riding a green horse. He bares an axe in one hand and a bough of Holly in the other. He states to all present that he will not fight any of them as they are all too weak, yet he has come to offer a Christmas game. The Green Knight, believed to have been a woodwose, challenged one person to strike him with his axe on the condition that one year and a day from then, that he can return and do the same. The axe would then belong to whoever accepts the challenge.

King Arthur is ready to accept the challenge, as no one else dared, however Sir Gwain (Arthur's nephew and a young knight but not yet a knight of the Round

Table) steps forward to accept the honour. The Giant bends over to bare his neck to Sir Gwain and with one stroke of the axe beheads him. To the shock of those present, the Green Knight picks up his severed head and climbs on to his horse. Showing his head to Queen Guinevere, he reminds the agreement made. The axe is then admired by all the Knights present and it is hung on the wall of the hall as a trophy.

Time passes and Sir Gwain travels to the agreed meeting place (the Green Chapel) where he will honour the challenge. It is mentioned that Sir Gwain had many battles and adventures during this time, but these are not described. Heading towards the Chapel, Sir Gwain comes across a magnificent castle where he meets the Castle's Lord and beautiful wife. Sir Gwain is welcomed, and he also noticed an old and ugly lady that is honoured at the castle. Sir Gwain talks about the challenge he faces, and this will take place in a few days' time. The Lord confirms there is a pathway to the chapel, so he can rest until he needs to go there.

The Lord proposes a friendly deal with Sir Gwain in order to make the next few days pass with reward. Each day, the Lord will go out hunting and will offer his prize in reward for whatever Sir Gwain had achieved on the same day. Seeing no harm in this deal, Sir Gwain agreed. On the first day, whilst the Lord was out hunting, the beautiful wife visits Sir Gwain in his room and tries to seduce him. Sir Gwain refuses her advances however he gained a single kiss from her. Upon returning from the hunt, the Lord gives Gwain a deer for his efforts and Gwain in turn gives the Lord a kiss, but does not reveal who this came from. The following day, the same takes place, but this time the wife gave Sir Gwain two kisses, which he then returns upon the Lord after his hunting trip. The prize this time was a wild boar. The third day, now getting closer to the day that he needs to depart, the wife calls upon Sir Gwain again. This time she tries her advances again and is denied, but not giving up, she offers Sir Gwain a gold ring. This was refused, so she pleads with him to accept her offer of her green sash made of green and gold silk. The sash, she explained, was charmed and would protect him from harm from his forthcoming challenge, but on the condition that he does not tell her husband. Willing to take any protection he could, Sir Gwain accepted the offer, and he received three kisses from the wife in the process. That evening, the Lord returned with a Fox and they exchanged their daily offerings….. but Sir Gwain only gave the Lord three kisses and kept quiet about the sash.

The following day Sir Gwain made his way to the Green Chapel, together with the sash around his waist. He sees the Green Knight waiting for him as he sharpens his axe. Bravely, Sir Gwain knelt down and bared his neck. On the first attempted swing Sir Gwain flinched slightly, which the Green Knight mocked him for. Ashamed for losing his nerve, on the second swing Sir Gwain did not flinch, but again, the Green Knight does not follow through with the blow of his axe. He explained that he was just testing his nerve.... But Sir Gwain's answer was to get on with it. The third attempt the Green Knight strikes but only causes a mild cut to the neck bringing an end to the challenge. Sir Gwain picks up his helmet, shield and sword and starts to walk away. The Green Knight laughs and then reveals himself as the Lord of the Castle and he was able to be transformed by magic by the old women, who was a sorceress, Morgan le Fay, who was King Arthur's stepsister. She had wanted to test King Arthur's Knights and to also scare Guinevere. Sir Gwain had only received the nick to his neck as he had concealed the truth about receiving the sash.

Remembering his deceit, Sir Gwain felt ashamed of himself, but the Green Knight just laughed and pronounces him as the most blameless Knight in the whole of Camelot. Upon returning, the Knights of the Round Table absolve him of blame and decide from that moment forward they would all wear a green sash in recognition of Sir Gwain's challenge and to act as a reminder for the virtue of being honest.

Man Monkey

Doing research over 12 years ago, I came across a book by Nick Redfern called 'Man Monkey' and it included a report from 1891 written by Charlotte S. Burne and Georgina F. Jackson about Shropshire Folklore. It relates to an incident that took place on the 21st of January, 1879 at the Bridge 39 canal bridge crossing the Shropshire Union Canal. It was around 10 o'clock at night and a cold and weary man was coming along the road with his cart and horse, then (quote):-

"Just before he reached the canal bridge, a strange black creature with great white eyes sprang out of the plantation by the roadside and alighted on his horse's back. He tried to push it off with his whip, but to his horror the whip went through the thing, and he dropped it on the ground in fright.

The poor, tired horse broke into a canter, and rushed onwards at full speed with the ghost still clinging to its back. How the creature at length vanished, the man hardly knew. He told his tale in the village of Woodseaves, a mile further on, and so effectively frightened the hearers that one man actually stayed with friends there all night, rather than cross the terrible bridge which lay between him and his home."

There are many other accounts of Wildman stories within the UK, including some that are relatively more modern.

Above & Below: The author standing on and next to bridge 39 across the Shropshire Union Canal.

Big Red of Sailsbury Plain

This incident relates to a report made in 2010 in reference to an encounter on Sailsbury Plain in the year 2002, eight years earlier. The witness was a British Army Tank Commander called George Price, who was on an exercise when he saw an approximate 6-foot-tall ape like creature run past his tank. It was running upright, like a human but with a different gait, it also had long reddish hair – similar to that of an Orangutan and with a darkish coloured face. His colleague who was also in the tank only saw it briefly but confirmed he did see something but not as well as George. Upon reporting this encounter to their superiors, like with many other encounters, this was just laughed off and not treated as anything credible. It took 8 years for George to come forward and report this incident in public.

There is little point in covering this further, it is just enough to confirm that there are stories within our earliest folklore, together with more modern stories. Some of these beliefs are set in stone! Just take a look at the Green Man carvings on Medieval churches. So, you just need to understand, just like in the more recent past where Gorillas were just labelled as myths, we need to keep an open mind behind the stories surrounding the Wildman.

Silvaticus

Above: Who is hiding in the woodlands? Who is invisible?

Silvaticus comes from the Latin words 'silva' (woods or forest) and 'aticus' meaning pertaining to /related to. Silvanus was a Roman God or Diety of the woods (and uncultivated lands). He would look over and protect the forests, animals and the likes, including farm animals from wolves, and he would also be responsible for promoting their fertility. Silvanus was understood to have been fond of music and the 'syrinx' (a pan flute) was sacred to him. Silvanus has been mentioned and being associated with Pan and Faunus. One of the other features that we should be aware of is the association that Silvanus has with the Roman God of War – Mars. **Marcus Porcius Cato** (234–149 BC), also known as **Cato the Censor** (*Censorius*), **the Elder** and **the Wise**, was the first person to write about Roman History in Latin – with the 'Origines' – a fragmentary historical record of Rome. Cato recorded repeatedly *'Mars Silvanus'* linking the two deities. The context here cannot be overlooked, as there is a potential link here with the art of forest warfare being evident.

So, how does this relate to the period that we are looking at related to Robin Hood? Well, potentially a lot. When the Normans invaded, they were not openly welcomed by the native Anglo-Saxons. You will have seen in earlier chapters the civil unrest and rebellions that took place following the Battle of Hastings, the draconian new laws introduced, and the harsh treatment of the people. There were many push backs with the Earls and Barons revolting. Norman Castles started popping up all over the place as strongholds. So, what did the Normans call these rebellious natives? You have probably got a good idea already – the **Silvatici!** The Anglo-Saxons engaged in guerrilla warfare by kidnapping Norman Nobles, attacking William's soldiers via ambushes as well as more major open battles/sieges. The Normans referred them as Silvatici as they were 'wild' and were 'from the forest'. To the English, it was the same, but were called 'the green men'.

According to an English/Norman chronicler, Orderic Vitalis (16 February 1075 – c. 1142), these men lived in rough tents in the wild, disdaining to live in houses lest they became soft.

You are probably now starting to understand the direction this is taking us…. However, this is a lot deeper than you can ever imagine…..

Above: The author holding a beautiful resident Robin that got trapped in a greenhouse, and then happily rescued – Summer 2023. First time ever holding a Robin. A coincidence?

The man behind the Legend?

Above: Did 'Robin' leave his mark in the history books?

Every legend has to have a starting point, correct? Every legend has to have a person that inspired the legend. Correct? Legends are, by definition, a traditional story, popularly regarded as historical but not authenticated. We accept that the tales of Robin Hood are considered part of a legend, in that it has basis for historical context, yet remains unauthenticated. Despite the many scholars that have investigated this, the starting point to the legend remains elusive.

But do any arrows from the past point us in a different direction?

So, with that in mind, it is with my greatest pleasure that I can introduce you to **Eadric.**

Eadric coming from old English 'ead' meaning 'riches or wealth' and 'ric' meaning 'ruler or leader.

Eadric was an Anglo-Saxon lord from Shropshire. Prior to the Norman Conquest, he held the position of thegn, which status was of a high-ranking nobleman, and second only to an ealdorman. He held vast portions of land in Shropshire and also some land in Herefordshire.

It is unknown, but unlikely, that Eadric fought William at Hastings, although there might have been chance that he was part of a flotilla of ships in the channel preventing William's force from being re-enforced (some evidence pointed to Eadric being the Bishop of Worcester's 'shipman'). However, there is no direct confirmation of this. What we do know is that once the Invasion had taken place, this put Eadric on a collision course with the Normans, who were slowly confiscating lands from the Saxon nobility. Had Eadric fought at the Battle of Hastings then he would have lost everything immediately. It is understood that following the confusion created by the Battle of Hastings in the South, two Norman Earls who already lived in the Welsh Marcherlands (invited over previously by Edward the Confessor), tried to extend their lands – including some of Eadric's estates, which caused bad blood and localised warfare.

Due to the passage of time and the disruption caused at this time, we are not fully aware of Eadric's pedigree. According to a 12th Century historian, John of Worcester, Eadric was the son of a man called Aelfric, who was also believed to have been related to Eadric Streona (a very important ealdorman of Mercia, serving under King Aethelred the Unready). Although it is uncertain, this relationship might place Eadric as a Grandson of Eadric Streona, giving rise to his link with nobility.

It would be safe to say that up until the autumn of 1066, Eadric would have had a very privileged life. As a result, the Norman Conquest caused a great period of upheaval and Eadric was not alone in suffering this fate. Following the invasion, and then the Norman Earl incursions, the majority of Eadric's manors were confiscated and then handed over to Norman lords who had helped William in his conquest. You can imagine then; Eadric did not take this order lightly and he resisted handing over his lands. Eadric's refusal was met with a brutal response, with his lands being laid waste. It is understood that Eadric faced the forces under Richard fitz Scrob, who was based at his castle stronghold at Hereford.

So, the year was 1067, only months following the Norman Invasion and Eadric became one of the first, if not the initial, of the revolutionists to Norman rule. This might have only been localised resistance, yet it sowed the seeds to bigger rebellions. Eadric teamed up with the Welsh prince of Gwynedd and Powys - Bleddyn ap Cynfyn and his brother – Rhiwallon ap Cynfyn. This act of rebellion was covered by the Anglo-Saxon Chronicle, by John of Worcester's Chronicle (an English monk and chronicler based at Worcester around this time) and also by Orderic Vitalis (a Benedictine Monk who wrote significant contemporary chronicles of this time period).

They attacked the Norman stronghold of Richard fitz Scrob at Hereford. They laid waste to the town, but could not overcome the Norman castle (most likely a Motte and Bailey type castle at this point, given these were first created in this area by the Normans already present (i.e. those invited by Edward the Confessor previously) and this was before the actual Norman Invasion). Given that Hereford castle had previously been destroyed by Welsh incursions in 1055, the new castle, being now strongly fortified meant that this attack proved unsuccessful. So, Eadric and his Welsh allies retreated to the Welsh Hills to plan their next moves.

This is where Eadric got his characteristic name of Eadric Silvaticus, Sylvaticus also known as Edric the Wild (Se Wilde), Wild Eadric, Eadric Cild or Child and Eadric the Forester (le Sauvage). Quite a list for an individual at this time, but it is what the Chroniclers and Norman's called him that sticks out – Eadric Silvaticus. The meaning of Silvaticus: 'Silva' is Latin meaning woods/forest, and 'ticus' meaning 'of ' or 'cause' (cus) of the woods. So, Eadric was clearly linked in this meaning. The Normans referred to these types of rebels or 'outlaws' collectively as Silvatici. They became the first representation of resistance by undertaking guerrilla warfare (invisible warfare) upon an invading force.

The Chronicler Orderic Vitalis describes the people of the English uprisings as living wild, many living in tents and refusing to live in houses should they 'become soft'. It was very clear from these accounts that the Silvatici were widespread during the years c.1068-9 when there were many rebellions made around the country. Many of these rebels would hide in woodlands, marshes and on islands to evade Norman soldiers. They would plunder and attack Norman forces and settlements where they could, which would certainly include roads and tracks – such as Watling Street (as mentioned as one of Robin Hood's own selected ambush places in early ballads). It should be noted that Watling Street (a former Roman Road connecting London with Holyhead, North Wales, now known as the A5) passes through Staffordshire and Shropshire, but does not pass directly through Nottinghamshire, although Staffordshire is an adjacent county to Nottinghamshire.

It should be known that during this time we get the name 'murdrum' or what we call murder now. This was a fine introduced by the new King William in order to help protect the arriving Norman settlers who had come to England. If a Norman was to be found killed and the killer was not known, then a murdrum fine was levied upon the inhabitants of the local area where the body was found, unless the murderer was brought to justice. Interestingly, there was no fine for any English people found to have been killed. You can imagine why this was required, as many Norman settlers would have turned up dead under mysterious circumstances and many of these would have related to the Silvatici, who, the English referred to as 'the Green Men'. Now, maybe this is where we get the idea of Robin Hood giving to the poor, in response to the severe penalties imposed upon the local inhabitants following the murdrum charge being applied following Silvatici attacks. It's possible, but there is another idea behind this saying, which we will look at later.

How effective were the Silvatici? Well, it became apparent that William's throne was not secure following the invasion, it would be over a decade before William gained some sense of control over all the lands. This invisible warfare was uncontrollable.

It was during the time of 1068-9 that the most intense rebel uprisings took place. In 1069 Eadric and his Welsh forces, together with rebels from Chester sacked the major town of Scrobbesburh, now called Shrewsbury, although they laid siege to the castle there, they could not overthrow it. Instead, the forces carried on sacking other Norman properties in the local area. At one point leading up to attacking Shrewsbury, they also burnt down a smaller castle in the Teme Valley, but reference to this is vague. The rebel forces then moved on towards another very important town - Chester.

At the time, William could do little to help matters as he was facing a bigger rebellion from the last remaining Wessex claimant to the English throne - Edgar Ætheling, who were amassing forces in Northern England. Edgar had been encouraging Anglo-Saxon, Northumbrian, Anglo-Scandinavian and Danish/Viking forces to rise up against William. This would have been William's most dangerous threat to his power and his campaigns in the North proved just how extreme his actions would be to subjugate the lands. William paid off the Danes to make them return home or move to other parts of the country, and when the remaining rebels refused to meet William in open battle, he then laid waste to the region. This was referred to as the 'Harrying of the North', or in layman's terms, considered to be the genocide of the population there (note: some refute this suggestion). William targeted the civilian population using a scorched earth policy during the winter of 1069/70 - cutting off supplies to the rebels. This took place primarily in Yorkshire, where it is thought at least 100,000 to 150,000 people died as a result of this campaign. William's forces were brutal, plundering and destroying everything they came into contact with. Due to the scotched earth policy, there was widespread famine that winter and many died. It is estimated, based upon figures from the Doomsday Survey, that up to 75% of the local population didn't survive, or return, following this episode. This was, in a word, an act of genocide recorded on British soil, and it is hard to imagine just how terrifying this period would have been after living decades of peace.

It was during William's campaigns in the North, that Eadric and the Welsh forces took advantage of the situation and tried to take the important town of Shrewsbury. Upon hearing of the sacking of the town, William, along with some of his elite forces turned his attention to crush this uprising and swiftly marched across the Pennine Hills to meet these rebels. Eadric was wary of the situation and probably aware of the numbers of forces coming to engage them, so he and his men from Shropshire and Staffordshire withdrew. This left the Welsh and other English forces to march on to fight, which happened at the Battle of Stafford (latter part of 1069), which William decisively won. However, Eadric was now in hiding in the hills and woodlands with his band of men.

Above: Modern day Cardiff Castle, Wales. The original fort built at this location was by the Romans in AD 55, then a series of forts and castles have been built upon this same spot since then. This included a Norman Motte and Bailey wooden castle shortly after 1066, but was then rebuilt in the 12th century by Robert of Gloucester and was then made from stone.

This defeat must have played heavy on Eadric's mind as in 1070 we understand that Eadric submitted to King William and then swearing fealty to him (according to the Chronicler Simeon of Durham). Following this, he even participated with William's invasion of Scotland in 1072. It is also recorded that Eadric campaigned for William in Maine, France also in 1072. I understood that William granted Eadric a small manor near Offa's Dyke (an Anglo-Welsh boundary dyke built in c.780), but he lost all of his extensive properties in Shropshire and Herefordshire.

However, there is another account that it was Ranulph de Mortimer 'after long struggles and handed over to the King for life imprisonment, some of his lands afterwards descending to the abbey' of Wigmore. Unfortunately, we do not know what led Eadric to be brought in front of the King leading him to swear fealty, but one thing is for certain and that is that Eadric formed some sort of mutual understanding, and a working arrangement going forward.

We know little of Eadric's life following this point; however, it was understood that he formed part of an uprising in 1075 during the Revolt of the Earls. This was a great threat to William and was caused by his attempts to reel in the powers of the Earls, as they were getting too powerful for William's liking. Three Anglo-Norman Earls revolted against William, yet it failed due to being betrayed by their co-conspirator Earl of Northumbria, when he revealed the whole plan to King William. Also, it lacked the appetite of the Anglo-Saxon population, as they now lived in fear of the consequences.

Eadric was known to have been actively involved with this revolt and according to genealogy, he held Wigmore Castle in Shropshire against Ranulph de Mortimer. Information regarding Eadric from this point forward are sparse or untenable, so is this where the story ends? Of course not.

There are various accounts about Eadric's past and the above are my own attempt in trying to make some sense of this. But we are looking for Robin Hood here, not an Eadric. Well, let's consider first what we have learnt about this legendary figurehead from the Anglo-Saxon/Norman period.

- Eadric was Anglo-Saxon
- Eadric was a nobleman, who became an outlaw.
- He had his estates taken from him by the Norman invaders.
- He fought guerrilla styled tactics to fight back against the Normans
- Watling Street passes through his area of Shropshire, in fact across Wigmore Moor.

- He gained the name 'Silvaticus' as he lived in the forests and planed his attacks from here.
- He had a band of warrior men who joined him.
- The Normans called them 'Silvatici', the English called them the 'Green Men'.
- Eadric eventually swore fealty to the new King William.
- Eadric served the King around 1072. Possibly for a couple of years.
- We have a link between Eadric and a Ranulph, but this Ranulph was not directly the Earl of Chester, but was still a Lord of the Marcherlands.

You can see that just by looking at the above we have some interesting overlaps with the classic stories behind Robin Hood. But yes, the name is Eadric and not Robin. This is located in Shropshire and Staffordshire and not Nottinghamshire. There is no Sheriff of Nottingham. There is no King John or Richard the Lionheart. So, let's carry on with the storyline behind Eadric Silvaticus, because there is more to tell.

Folklore stories

Robin Hood is a folklore story that has been passed down through the ages due to oral traditions, eventually ending up being recorded in the fifteenth century. What we know about oral traditions is that they change over time and the longer the period of time, then more further from the truth the oral traditions become. Remember, their purpose is to relate to the receptive populations they are aimed at, at that time. The earliest reference we have from Robin Hood is from 1377 which implies that the stories behind Robin Hood were well known and talked about amongst the people. Now, do you think that the ruling Normans would accept open celebrations on May Day in recognition of a rebellious character such as Eadric? A person, who from Day 1, acted as a force of defiance to Norman dominance? Of course not. So, lets now take a look at the known folklore stories behind Eadric from Shropshire.

In true Arthurian tradition, there is a legend that there is a giant fish of Bomere Pool that still carries the sword of Wild Edric. The sword is strapped to the side of the fish, and no one has ever been able to catch it. At one point it was netted, but it used the sword to cut itself free. Faced with this failure, the fisherman used a net made of iron links and managed to catch it and bring ashore, only for the fish to use the sword again to cut itself free and return to the water. This shocked all the local people who never attempted to catch it again. It was occasionally seen in the shallows of the pond still brandishing the sword.

The story behind this is that Eadric was fishing at the pond (and he may have been connected to the local Manor of Condover, even born there) and they hooked this massive fish and landed it. Eadric and his friend disputed the size of the fish, so Eadric took off his sword and scabbard and wrapped it around the fish and it fitted! Naturally, the fish escapes including the sword and scabbard wrapped around it. The lore is that the fish will only release the sword to the true heir to Condover Manor, given this would have been confiscated by the Normans.

Other stories tell that Eadric's sword was placed in the pool on the heath, Bomere Pool, ready for another day when Eadric will return to collect it and wield it once more in battle. It was protected by a magical fish that will safeguard it until Eadric needs it again. This sounds very much like the tale of King Arthur and the sword in the lake. Certainly, during this time period swords were given as ritual offerings to rivers and lakes as a means of appeasing the gods. This is another element to do with Eadric that links in with powerful legends, in a similar vein to the stories surrounding King Arthur.

Is that it? No.

Walter Map (c. 1140 – 1209) was one of the Court Clerics to Henry II. He was born near Hereford so would have been familiar regarding the stories surrounding Eadric. Around 1180 he wrote 'De Nugis Curialium' (the book of Courtier's Trifles) regarding stories, some supernatural in style, that would appeal to the royal court at times of relaxation. A couple of these relate to Eadric the Wilde.

In summary, Eadric was a strong man that lived up to his reputation of 'the Wild' yet he was also a fair man and never misused his rights.

His joys in life were spending fun nights with his friends whilst drinking and merrymaking. His other joy was hunting. He loved to hunt around the Slipperstones, Long Mynd and through the Forest of Clun.

One hot day he was out hunting with friends and towards the end of the day along came a refreshing evening breeze. He told his hunting party to make their own way back to the manor house at Lydbury North. Eadric made his own way back, but he noticed there was some music being carried upon the breeze. Was it his imagination? Yet his horse also started to prick its ears to the sounds, which started to become clearer. He then directed the horse to follow the sound of the music.

They ended up at a clearing in the forest with a small, strange cottage that Eadric had never seen before. The music was coming from the cottage, so he dismounted and peered through a window. To his surprise he saw six beautiful maidens dancing around a seventh, who was the most beautiful of all. At that moment he was filled with love for her, and he wanted her for his bride. Given he was the Lord of the land, he had rights to enter, which he did, seizing the maiden around the waist he then tried to make off with her. As he did, the remaining six beautiful maidens turned into wild and savage beasts. Eadric then used his sword to fight them off as he moved towards the door. Getting out of the cottage he threw the girl over the back of the horse and then climbed on and took off at speed with the six beasts close behind. He galloped off then losing them in the forest.

Upon reaching Lydbury Hall, the maiden calmly walked into the Great Hall and sat down and watched cautiously as Edric followed. She sat at that same spot sitting silently all day and possibly all night. It wasn't until the third day that she spoke.

'I know who you are – you are Eadric, the one they call the Wild' she said. She had watched and learned about Eadric and saw him as a straight and true person, and not 'wild' at all. She knew that he wanted to marry her, and she agreed to allow him – but he needed to understand who she was first.

'I am Godda and I am Queen of the Fairy Folk', she then explained that Eadric had stolen her from her six sister fairies. She agreed to marry him and live her life as a human, provided he never 'reproached' her. Reproach her, due to her and her sisters being fairies, or where he found her and where he stole her from. Should he do so, then she will return to the Fairy World.

Eadric swore an oath to Godda on this basis and then the two of them were wed. They were the finest couple in the land, and everyone knew of Godda, his fairy wife.

Word eventually got around to King William, who Eadric had previously fought, but had now made peace. So, the King invited them both to his Court and there he declared that they were indeed the finest couple of the Kingdom. He invited them both to stay, but the draw of the Shropshire Hills were beckoning, so they returned to Lydbury North. Here they lived happily and had a son called Alned. Unfortunately, Eadric could not keep to his word. Godda was late serving his breakfast one morning and in a fit and rage he spoke 'Where have you been wife? Was it your sisters that kept you from me?' Thinking instantly about what he had just said, he realised that he had broken his oath, but it was too late – Godda just disappeared and he never saw her again.

From this point forward, he became truly wild. He would spend days searching for his beloved Godda, but he did not find her and he died not long after as a broken man. That said, to this day, his ghost still continues to ride the Shropshire hills in search of his beloved wife.

Many have seen the hunt, and some say that he has been reunited with Godda, as they have both been seen riding together. The sight of the 'Hunt' is also seen as a precursor to war.

This story also links in with the idea that the Anglo-Saxon people of the time were not happy that Eadric had sworn allegiance to William, so he was taken prisoner and locked away in the mines of the Shropshire Hills, but was cursed to remain there until England had been returned to normality like it was before the Norman Invasion. It is said that the spirit of Eadric, Godda and a band of his men can be seen/heard galloping across the Shropshire moors when England is faced with adversity/war and that the ghosts are charging in the direction from where the threat was to come from. Documented accounts of this range from just prior to the Crimean War, together with prior to the first and second World Wars. Eadric is seen dressed all in green with a cloak and a cap with a white feather. He had a sword at his side and carried a horn with him. Lady Godda had long blonde hair that reached her waist. She had a white headband and carried a dagger in her belt.

You can see that these visions of Eadric riding across the moorlands links in with other visions around different parts of Europe that relate to the 'Wild Hunt', where ghostly apparitions are seen riding on horseback. They all symbolise something, but cannot all be relative to the same person. So, what can we gain from these folklore stories from Shropshire?

Clearly these stories follow previous held beliefs, legends or stories of old. The sword in the lake mirrors those ideas related to King Arthur. The 'Wild Hunt' stories can be traced back further in time, and maybe linked to the Norse God Odin (God of War and Death). So, a character like Eadric being associated with such stories must prove that he was an important character at this unsettling time. Did people really see these hordes of warriors racing towards a foreign threat? We do not know, but the same theme appears in different countries and probably for similar reasons. All these stories originated from somewhere.... and for some purpose.... and that is the beauty of legends, we are not in a position to nail down the starting point, yet they meant something to the people of a bygone age.

Now we can take a look at the story behind Eadric and Godda – his fairy bride. Quite a story and one that we have difficulty believing – correct? I would tend to agree with this. Eadric is mortal after all and marrying a fairy would be monumental. But in this age of superstition, fairies were very real, and many stories abound regarding their interactions with humans. We have already touched upon one very famous story from Greek/Roman times about the union between a human bride and a God. You will recall that we touched upon the story behind Eros and Psyche. Eros being the Greek God and Cupid being the Roman God.

Now we are starting to look for reasons how these folklore stories came about. Remember at the time of the Norman Conquest, the language spoken and written heavily included Latin. It might have been 800 years since the Romans departed Britain, yet its influences lasted long after their leaving. Needless to say, their stories and legends would have had influence upon those people responsible for recording historical references and as we know, this was done in such a way that it appealed to the audience. This is where our knowledge is at the mercy of the Chroniclers of the time. Some would have been written as historical fact, others loosely connected to truth, and some that are pure fantasy or fiction. And we can see that the birth of Robin Hood probably followed a combination of those paths. But let's take a look at Eros again. What do we know about Eros – well, he was one of the primeval Gods, son of the first ever God, the God of Chaos. Eros was the God of love and fertility. He was an archer, and his arrows could change the course of destiny. He was invisible. He could fly with his wings, much like an angel. He fell in love with a beautiful mortal woman who had to follow considered impossible trials in order succeed with her challenges. She achieved these, despite all the odds stacked up against her.

We can see that Eadric fell in love with the queen of the fairies. A very important and influential being to the people of this period. The link between the fairy world and that of mankind speaks volumes. Eadric was accepted by the Fairy Queen and even bore a child with him. The fairy world was considered very powerful, and the people of the day would leave out bread and milk to appease the good nature of the fairies. The fairies were magical beings with abilities that were off the scales to the normal person. Were these beliefs unfounded? That's for later, but what we must consider here is that stories from Roman legends most likely influenced the narrative – as with Eadric, as with Robin Hood. Where is this leading us to then?

Let's try and break it down a bit.

- Eadric was associated with the forests – Silvaticus – 'of the forest'.
- The fairy world is linked with the forests – enchanted forests, where Robin is also linked.
- Eadric legends suggests that he had links with the fairy world.
- Eadric was labelled as one of the 'Green Men', and the fairies were all dressed/associated with green and nature.
- Robin Hood was said to be dressed in green (Lincoln Green).
- The fairy world is linked with the May Day Celebrations.
- Robin Hood is linked with the May Day Celebrations.
- The green man is associated with the May Day Celebrations – e.g. Jack in the Green.
- Maid Marion (although a later addition) is considered in Pagan tradition as the goddess of Spring, the flower goddess or the Queen of the Fairies and would be chosen for her natural beauty. She would become the bride of Robin Hood.
- Legend has it that Eadric married the beautiful Fairy Queen - Godda.
- Legend has it that Eros married a beautiful mortal human bride.
- The May Day celebrations are linked with fertility and love.
- The May Day celebrations are also linked with 'hope' – hope for the future, be it harvests, love or general well-being.
- Eros is linked with fertility and love. Eros is the offspring of Chaos. Out of Chaos comes love.
- Eros/Cupid are both archers. Robin Hood was an archer. Eadric was most likely an archer too if doing hit and run concealed attacks. They all became masters of invisibility.
- Eros (i.e. love) was one of the first Greek Gods and it is said that he was the fairest amongst the immortal gods, and he conquers the minds and thoughts of all gods and men. He could change destiny. Cupid had two different tipped arrows – one for love, the other for changing people's minds/destiny.
- Psyche was set trials as part of the story with Eros, Robin Hood stories are all about 'trials'.
- Heard the expression that Love conquers all? 'Omnia Vincit Amor' – written around 37 BC.
- Folklore legends regarding Eadric are just stories. Folklore legends regarding Eros are just stories. Folklore legends regarding Robin Hood are just stories. There is no factual basis and accuracy behind these folklore stories. They are, to a certain extent, made up to suit the audience they are aimed at. But what would have been the driving force behind said stories?

- Eadric Silvaticus, or Edric the Wild was a real person. He acted as the first resistance to Norman rule and probably inspired further rebellions. He hid in the forests as an outlaw. He was labelled by the English as a 'Green Man'. He most likely inspired various stories, yes, likely those of Robin Hood.
- The Green Man. There is another take upon the green man, also known as the 'Wildman'. They are the spirits of the forest and associated with the fairy world. They were also called Woodwusa. They are often depicted as stone or wooden carvings upon Churches and Cathedrals built during this period. They were symbolic and likely carried a double meaning behind their existence.

You will probably see that there are some connections there, but these all seem random and the connection between Robin and Eadric are not yet very clear. This is understandable, but we will now try and draw all of this together and you are in for a bit of a mindblower.

Robin Goodfellow

For he's a Jolly Good Fellow, for he's a Jolly Good Fellow, for he's a Jolly Good Fellow, and so say all of us! (British version) and 'which nobody can deny' (American version). I'm sure many of you have heard this before and even sung it in recognition of someone you know achieving something important. The funny thing is that this melody originated in France, believed following the Battle of Malplaquet in 1709 and was referred to as "Marlborough s'en va-t-en guerre". It became a very popular folk tune in France as Marie Antoinette became interested in it after hearing one of her maids singing to the future King Louis XVII, which helped promote its popularity.

Given this popularity at the time, it became part of one of Beethoven's greatest compositions – Wellington's Victory (written 1813). Also referred to as the 'Battle of Vitoria' or 'Battle Symphony' – which used real musket and cannon fire within the music! This was to commemorate the Battle of Vitoria (in Spain, 21 June, 1813), where the Duke of Wellington's victory over Joseph-Napoléon Bonaparte brought an end to Napoleon's rule of the Rhine Confederation. It was dedicated to the Prince Regent, later to be King George IV and celebrated a turn in European geopolitics. The two sides of the battle were represented by 'Rule Britannia' for the British forces and 'Marlborough s'en va-t-en guerre' representing the French forces. The symphony was once described as a "sonic assault on the listener" given the loudness of the music and instruments used. Since Wellington's win at Waterloo (1815), the symphony has lost its appeal, yet as we know, the melody associated with this has remained popular to this day.

This may seem odd to include this here, but I feel it is worth noting that a) you can appreciate the initial meaning behind the melody has been lost over time, yet it is still a very popular melody, even to this day. Traditions do clearly carry on, even if we have lost the logic behind its original source. And b) the words used resonate a very powerful meaning behind it. A 'Jolly Good Fellow' is an old-fashioned term for a very popular person.

Let's now look at the context for this character from Medieval history. Some will already recognise that Robin Goodfellow was a character used in one of Shakespeare's famous plays – a Mid-Summer Nights Dream. Robin is known better as Puck in the play. Puck is described as a fairy, a brownie or demon (medieval lore), or a hobgoblin – a magical forest sprite. He is portrayed as a jester for Oberon, the King of the Faries. Shakespeare portrays him as a trickster but also making errors which lead to comical consequences. His most famous line from the play appears in Act 3 – 'Lord, what fools these mortals be'. For most people, past and present, the true meanings behind this character have been lost over time – as this is just meant to be a made-up character for the sake of the story. That said, this is a very deep subject – which, I will be honest, took me over 10 years of research to throw some light upon. The meanings behind Robin Goodfellow are now evident and yet, the truth was already there, recorded hundreds of years ago!

So where did Shakespeare get the name 'Puck' from? Well, as you appreciate from the play, Puck was a woodland sprite, and his name comes from the Celtic/old English name of Puca – meaning 'goblin'. Various words such as púca, pwca, pooka, phouka, puck relate to the same thing from Irish, English, Celtic and Channel Island records. Puck is also referred to as a Hobgoblin – this maybe where the prefix Robin came from – 'Rob', and Rob being short for Robin, which in itself comes from the name Robert. You can now start to appreciate this better, as Hob used to be the short name for Hobgoblin, which we now refer to as 'Bob' – and 'Bob' being a short name for Robert. These are all linked! Now, Hobgoblin was reference to a demon in old English folk lore. So, this is all getting rather complex now, but we can start to see that there are some hidden meanings behind some names and characters as seen in Shakespeare's plays, but one thing is evident, Robin Goodfellow was associated with a forest sprite/ demon/ hobgoblin etc.

Above: Robin Goodfellow, as portrayed in the Mad Pranks and Merry Jests of Robin Goodfellow, 1639. Notice any similarities to other historical or religious characters?

So how can Robin Goodfellow be linked to Robin Hood? Well, we are already aware of the link between Robin Goodfellow and the green man, but how far back do the stories about Robin Goodfellow go back to. Well, it would appear that the earliest references date back to the 13th Century housed in the Bodleian Library in Oxford. It is also referenced (MS Digby, No. 172, in the Foreign Quarterly Review, 1836-10: Volume 18, Issue 35. P. 189) that Robinet, or Robin, seems to have the characteristics of a Hobgoblin (the below represents a modern translation of the Latin version):

> *'Once Robinet was in a certain house in which certain soldiers were resting for the night, and, after having made a great clamour during the*

better part of the night, to their no small annoyance, he was suddenly quiet. Then said the soldiers to each other, 'Let us now sleep, for Robinet himself is asleep.' To which Robinet made reply, 'I am not asleep, but am resting me, in order to shout the louder after.' And the soldiers said, ' It seems, then, that we shall have no sleep to-night.' So sinners sometimes abstain for a while from their wicked ways, in order that they may sin the more vigorously after-wards .... The soldiers are the angels about Christ's body, Robin is the devil or the sinner'.

It is also noted that Henry Chettle was in the process of writing, or did actually write, a play about Robin Goodfellow in September 1602, which would be 2 years following Shakespeare's Midsummer Night's Dream. This is shown in the below account from his diary

> "Lent unto harey Chettell the 7 of Septmbr 1602, at the apoyntment, to lend in earenest of a tragedie called Robin hoodfellowe, some of ⎫ s
> ⎬ x
> ⎭
>
> " Lent unto harey chettell the 9 of Septembr 1602 in pt of payment of a playe called Robingoodfellowe, some of ⎫ s
> ⎬ x
> ⎭

Well, it would appear that a sum of money was lent to a Harey Chettell on September 7th and 9th in reference to Robin hoodfellowe and then again to Robingoodfellow... was this pure coincidence? Or are the two plays that are referenced here at the same time in fact actually linked to the one and same play? Robin Hood and Robin Goodfellow are connected? This seems to be too much of a coincidence, and it does also link in with later ideas.

Above: The book that initially sent the author on this journey of discovery – the Mad Pranks and Merry Jests of Robin Goodfellow (1639). Given the seasons played an important role in the first book, this was a picture of the book resting upon a Neolithic aged Polisher stone on Fyfield Down, Wiltshire. This is the location where some of the stones from Stonehenge were retrieved from, and these marks in this stone were likely made by the builders, sharpening their axes in order to cut down trees for the rollers for transporting the stones.

ROBIN HOOD: SILVATICI

Above: Robin Goodfellow, as the Wildman, 1639.

Above: Do these two characters represented here look similar to Robin Goodfellow?

Loxley or Lockersley? Again…

We have already mentioned other possibilities behind the name of Lockersley being mentioned in association with Robin Hood, but is there any real truth behind it or is it made up, just like a lot of the stories were? I don't know, but there was potentially a reason behind the name being referenced and a hint at the truth.

Well, when we turn our attention to Wild Eadric, then we understand that there is a Lockley Wood in Shropshire. This woodland has all disappeared now, but by taking a look at the below map from the late 1600s (from Robert Moredon's map that was included within William Camden's 'Britannia') you can see this area was heavily forested in bygone days. Folklore suggests that Eadric was born near to Bomere Pool at a place called Condover Manor, which is just to the south of Shrewsbury. Now, this location is around 22 miles from Lockley Wood, yet within Lockley Wood, as seen in this historical map, there is a place called 'Childs Arcol' – modern day name being 'Childs Ercall'. Now, one of the names that Wild Eadric had was Eadric 'Cild' or 'Child' - yet the reason for this name is totally unknown, but was thought to relate to his title rank, but that seems very odd. However, could Eadric Child be linked to the location here? And yes, in the middle of Lockley Wood? The name 'Child' has confused academics as to its meaning relative to Eadric. Maybe this is it then.

Does Arcol come from the Greek 'Archalou' – a sacred place of the nymphs?

We also understand that a locative byname (surname linked to a location) was a common way in the Medieval period to link a person to a place. When we previously looked at the potential hidden meaning behind Lockersley, we found that it could represent a 'bolt hole within a forest clearing'. Now take a look at the map…. Is Child Arcol a settlement set within a forest? Was this the link we have been looking for? And Eadric basing his resistance from this forest and obtaining the name Eadric Child fit in with this idea? Is this where the legend of Robin Hood was 'born'?

Naturally, I have no way of being able to say if this is linked, or not linked, but yet again, it is another coincidence that may need closer scrutiny by others going forward, but it does add more weight to the idea that is being proposed.

Above: Map of the area of Lockley Wood, with a particular reference. Remember, this was a map from the late 1600's, so this was likely an isolated settlement at the time period we are looking at.

Above: Map of Shropshire by Robert Mordon c.1695. You can see the area of Lockley Wood towards the upper right of the map, and the reddish area near the centre is Shrewsbury. Notice how heavily forested the area is around Lockley compared to other areas, but this was around 1695, yet the area is still heavily forested.

Bringing it all together....

We understand that English history is complicated, there are too many gaps that remain unfilled, particularly when it comes to the 11th Century. This was a time 500 years before the printing press, and a time when very few people could read and write. There was also no standardised language. The people of the time were very superstitious and just about every tale told would have been through oral tradition or acted out in plays. The Norman Invasion had created a very turbulent time following over 150 years of relative peace. The people did not ask for this change, nor did they want it. It was a period of great upheaval with new laws and overlords. The backdrop was set for a hero that will save the day and restore things to the way they were. Surely, if there was ever a character who would stand up to the Normans, then now was the right time.

In the previous chapter you have seen one character that really ticks a lot of the boxes that could relate to the Legend of Robin Hood, yet this appears much earlier than the ballads suggest. Does this matter? In all honesty, no, it doesn't. There are no factual records that link Robin to the time of Richard the Lionheart and the earliest reference in 1377 does not mention the time period in question. So, 1066 through to 1377 is a very long time – over 300 years. Now that is a very long time for stories told orally to be twisted and reinvented to suit the new narrative of the day. Just look at how Robin and his stories changed between 1377 and 1577 – just 200 years. So, could the person we have looked at, Eadric the Wild, Eadric Silvaticus, be the real person behind the legend? I believe so, yet where is the link to the name?

This is where it gets complicated and you are going to have to have an open mind here and yes, just trust me. My involvement in this subject did not come from my specific interest in Robin Hood, although, like most people, there is a general interest and admiration for the qualities that Robin promotes. Yet I never delved into this until the end of 2023. However, my own journey over the last 10 years has led me here and this directly follows on from my previous book. I have kept the subject related to this fairly quiet so far, and for obvious reasons, as the world is not ready to deal with it.... yet for the last 10 years I have been trying to make sense of it all myself. The topic? Well, in the UK we call him the Green Man, Woodwose, or the Wild Man, and around the world he is known under many different names – including Bigfoot. Yes, Bigfoot. For the last 10 years I have been following up on reports related to the UK Bigfoot and what can I say, it is no fantasy or myth, they are real. I have seen them personally, yet they are far more complex than just a missing link, far, far, far more complex. Hence my previous book – 'Bigfoot – It's a Fairy Tale'. The book covers my 10 year journey leading up to some revolutionary outcomes. Not only does it confirm that we are not the only intelligent life force on this planet, but it also confirms that life, as we know it, is far more complex than just carbon-based life forms. It also confirms that our ancestors were well aware of the existence of these beings living in the forests. And what was the Roman name for the forest beings? Well, it was 'Silvanus' - the Roman God of the Woodlands. Are you detecting a link here yet?

Let's carry on with this. If you read my previous book, then you will see that English folklore is tied into this, with Shakespeare even incorporating one of his key characters within the play – A Midsummer Night's Dream. This was 'Puck', a woodland sprite and the offspring of Oberon (King of the Faeries) and a human 'Damsell – neat and faire'. Puck gets his name from an old English word - Puca – meaning Goblin. Can you remember a similar story related to a Roman/Greek God and a human? Can you also recall an English folklore story following a similar vein? Interesting... but do you also know what Puck's real name was? Well, it is 'Robin Goodfellow'. The story behind Robin Goodfellow is yet again shrouded in mystery, but he can certainly be traced back further than Shakespeare's time and is always linked to the fairy world. It was well known that the fairies would do good deeds to those who deserved it yet would play tricks upon those that did bad. Hence the name 'Good-fellow'. To appease the fairy folk, people would leave out bread and milk as an offering so that they were good to the household. Can you think of any other long-standing tradition that we still do today every year that follows that practice? Well, that is what the other book talks about, backed up by historical reference, but I am certain you are already putting two and two together here. And, you might be interested to learn that the two are connected. But let's carry on with our theories here.

Above: Seleukid Kingdom Antiochos VII Euergetes 138-129 BC. Including a winged Eros (the wings are just about seen at the bottom left).

Eros, the Greek God of Love or Cupid, the Roman God of Love stand out here. Are both of these characters represented as archers using a bow and arrow? Does the legend of Eros include the God falling in love with a human woman of incredible beauty? Does the legend involve quests? Yes, it does and this all links in with the legends surrounding Eadric and there is some overlap here with Robin Hood. After all, why is Robin Hood associated with the May Day festivities? Why does he marry the May Queen, Queen of the fairies? It does seem odd that an outlaw would end up being celebrated in such a way, other than it having roots with other held ideas linked to folklore tales. And I think we are starting to see that link grow stronger and stronger here. The May Day festivities date back generations and would have been a time of celebration, a time of happiness and also a time of 'hope' for the new harvest season and the future. Certainly, there were similar celebrations held during Roman times and indeed, the symbol of the May Pole is believed to date back to this period, where Romans would dance around a decorated tree. There is also reference to fairies here, as dancing around the May Pole was related to Fairy Rings. We also have Jack in the Green – an association with the Green Man. These traditions are still very much alive today, so folklore stories might change over time, yet traditions repeat themselves every year. Take a look at the idea of leaving out bread and milk on Christmas Eve. Old habits die hard as they say. Remember that Robin Hood games were associated with the May Day festivals and the first being recorded in 1426 in Exeter, yet it is very likely that these took place way before this date too.

So, May Day was a time to celebrate fertility, love, and hope. A very powerful and important time within the Medieval Calendar. Some traditions would see the night before the celebrations having couples disappear into the glades for the night and attend the celebrations in the morning carrying flowers or whitethorn blossom. This is exactly why it is called the Merry, Merry Month of May! It was a time of fun, frolicking and merriment. Indeed, there was even a Robin Hood's arbour where lovers could attend during the May Day festivities for some 'quiet time'. Robin himself was the Summer Oak King and his beautiful partner being the Queen of May, or Maid Marion. This part of the tradition still lives on to modern times where a May Day Queen is crowned. Maid being reference to an unmarried lady – and where you get the term Maiden name. And usually, the May Queen is chosen for her youth and beauty – just like the Queen of the Fairies. It is also easy to see why Robin Hood's men were then called the 'Merry Men'.

You will also notice that a lot of Green Men carvings in churches have him represented surrounded by oak leaves and/or acorns. In essence this is linking the Green Man with the Oak Summer King (alongside fertility), and as we already know, this was also reference to Robin Hood. So, are the sculptures represented within Medieval, particularly 11th and 12th century Churches and Cathedrals a direct, yet disguised, reference to Robin Hood and the undertones to resistance to the Norman rule? Was this propaganda set in stone left by the defeated, yet still defiant Anglo-Saxon people? Were people reminded of this every Sunday when attending church and making their prayers, prayers of hope? I cannot help but feel that this is the case. Either way, it had a double meaning, just like the May Games, a link with the green man and with the other green man – Robin. You can now imagine how important the May Day celebrations became.... It was a time of 'hope' for the future, a time to call out to the Wildman of the woods to use their hidden powers. Remember that Robin Goodfellow played tricks or served justice on bad people yet rewarded the good people. Was this a time to call for their help to rid the destructive Norman invaders? Was that the same measures employed by the creators of the Green Men carvings within the churches – where people also prayed for their help?

This is all fascinating and potentially linked, but how can we say if Eadric was the real man behind the legend. The man that gave hope to the people of England during this time of turbulence, a man that will restore the old traditional values to the majority Anglo-Saxon people. Well, this is where my own research into the Wild man of England kicks in and you will have to read my first book to understand my journey to reach this point. So, to cut things short, I will just have to say that the wild man of England is real, very real. I coined them the name Anglosasquatch many years ago. I thought that name was appropriate, and you can trace some of my journey on youtube – on the channel sharing the same name. I started out with the idea that the encounters made by other people historically were mistaken identity or just made-up stories. But over 10 years ago when I first started researching, some forest features did not make any sense and some of these features followed perceived Bigfoot like activity in the USA, so my interest intensified. I got a friend involved (Ricky) and on our second nighttime visit on the 9th of July, 2015 we gained the proof that convinced us that they are real. Ever since that night, our adventures and experiences have just been overwhelming and has turned our understanding of the world upside down. So, you can imagine what medieval people once thought...and why there are so many stories abound about these Wild men and fairies. At first, we were looking for a missing link type of hominid, yet certain things associated with the Wild men were clearly out of the ordinary and we could not explain them. We were seeing balls of lights floating around the forest at nighttime and electrical items turning off or on by themselves. We were being touched by **invisible** forces and smelling things in the forest that made no sense. We had the feelings of electricity in the air, feelings of euphoria (and on a couple of occasions, feelings of dread).... and after a few years I received messages. How? This is best described in my book, but in the Bigfoot community it is called 'mind-speak' (telepathic messaging) and this is all labelled the 'woo'. For a long time, the mainstream Bigfoot community would dispel this as rubbish, yet only in 2024, that appears to have changed. My book published in 2023 might have had some influence upon this, I don't know, but clearly there has been a seismic change in understanding. On the 9th of April, 2024 Matt Moneymaker from the Bigfoot Field Researchers Organisation (BFRO), founder of the group and the team leader of the popular American TV series 'Finding Bigfoot', opened up saying that he can no longer suppress all of the accounts linking weird 'woo' like activity in association with Bigfoot. For me, I had been talking about this for years and we were called nutters in the many Facebook Bigfoot Groups for even mentioning this. So, for me, my last book was a mind blower to many people, but at last the mainstream Bigfoot groups are now opening up to the whole paranormal side to these beings. OK, so that was a long story cut short, now is the time to explain some of the things that has blown my own mind away. I'll try to explain this now, but you will need to clear your mind regarding everything that you have been educated on to date, as this is going to test your whole belief system.

You will recall me saying about balls of light flying through the forests at nighttime. These are referred to as 'Willow-the-wisp' in many accounts, both historically and more recently. You will understand that it is no coincidence that the people in the past would refer to them as fairies and associated with the faerie-world. I think Tinker-bell in Peter Pan is a good analogy to how you might see them flying around in the distance, and what people once imagined them to be and now you know why Fairies have wings and are glowing! Naturally, if you have never seen one, then you are none the wiser. My book confirms just how many times I have seen them, but on the best night I witnessed over 300 orbs of light, in the space of just a few hours, all within around 6 feet of me. Yes, like I said, you need an open mind in following my line of thought here, but I can assure you that I am telling the truth here.

Above: A Christmas decoration of a fairy sitting upon a glass ball, which looks very similar to the way we see orbs in the forest (without the fairy on top).

As I also mentioned above, I was able to mind speak with these forest people and back in 2017 I was asked by a friend to find out the name of the wild man or Bigfoot seen and filmed on the 20th October, 1967 at Bluff Creek, California. It is the most famous footage of what is understood to be a Wildman/Bigfoot/Sasquatch. Surprisingly, I was given the name Enrith by my forest person contact. I repeatedly asked and got the same answer again and again. Interesting, but an odd name I thought. It was about a month later that I checked if the name carried any hidden meaning to it and given that Hebrew had appeared in the names of some of my mind speak contacts, then I looked up what the name meant in Hebrew. This is where the mystery dawned on me. Erith in Hebrew means 'flower'. So, I went back and asked if it was Enrith or Erith and was told it is the same, same name and same meaning. Only now do I understand that significance when it comes to looking at Robin, Robyn, or Robert etc. This would become meaningful later when I was trying to join the dots behind Robin Hood.

But before we go there... the earliest mention of Robin Hood also includes a character, Randolf, Earl of Chester... let's turn the hand lens upon this character first, because he doesn't appear in any of the later ballads.

Above: Artistic reproduction of the Green Man /Oak King of Summer.

Randolph, Earl of Chester

So, thinking back to earlier references, what came first – the chicken or the egg? Well, you will appreciate that the earliest origin to that question carries more substance in answering it. So, in 1377, the earliest reference to Robin Hood, when he is mentioned in the 'Visions of Piers Plowman' by William Langland – there is a reference alongside Robin - 'I do not know my paternoster' as the priest recalls. 'But I do know rhymes of Robin Hood and Randolf, earl of Chester'. So, let's take another look at this person - Randolf. Needless to say, history has not given us any clear references to this person (just like Robin), other than the Earl of Chester. The ballads in relation to this individual have long since been lost. If they were told orally, then these were never transferred on to paper. I believe I can understand why this was, but let's try and work out who this person was and what relevance, if any, has he got associated with the tales of Robin Hood. To scholars, I believe they must think he is just an historical person, unrelated to the story, yet I believe that he is in fact, key. Unfortunately, history doesn't leave us all the answers that we demand, it is a jigsaw puzzle, and we must try and join all the pieces for it to make sense. If we take it from Piers Plowman, the ballads associated with these two people are intertwined, then who was this Randolf, Earl of Chester?

The Earldom of Chester was one of, if not, the most powerful earldoms in medieval England. Indeed, Prince William is the current Earl of Chester and Catherine is the Countess of Chester. This is due to King Henry III understanding that Cheshire was so powerful and important that he transferred the title of Earl of Chester to the Crown. It was then in 1254 that Henry's son, King Edward I, gave the lands of the Earldom of Chester to his own son – Edward – who then became the first Prince of Wales. Following this, the title of the Earl of Chester has remained with the Price of Wales ever since, and with this, confirming who is next in line to the throne.

We can now appreciate just why Chester was such an important place during Norman times. Indeed, King John even set aside Cheshire in the Magna Carta, as he believed the Earl of Chester could issue his own version of the document. So, let's now take a look at the Norman Earls of Chester and see if any of them are relative to what we are after.

The first Earl of Chester was Gerbod the Flemming in 1067. It is understood that he was taken prisoner in France whilst fighting there and dies in captivity in 1070. William the Conqueror then gave the position to his nephew, Hugh D'avranches or more commonly known as Hugh Lupus (Hugh the wolf) in 1071 (until 1101).

There was a total of 8 Norman Earls of Chester, the ones following Hugh are:

Richard D'avranches -	1101 – 1120
Ramulf le Meschin -	1120 – 1129
Ramulf de Gernon -	1129 – 1153
Hugh de Kevelioc -	1153 – 1181
Ranulf de Blideville -	1181 – 1232
John the Scot -	1232 – 1237

We do have a Ranulf in 1181 (Ranulph de Blideville or Blondeville), and this is the one that scholars believe relates to the story of Robin Hood. So why is this? Ranulf was a loyal follower of the Angevin Dynasty (the Angevin Kings of England, meaning coming from 'Anjou' in France, and include Henry II, Richard I, and John (from 1153 to 1216). Ranulf was a traditional Anglo-Norman Baron and described as one of the last relics of the great feudal aristocracy of the Norman Conquest. He ruled the area with an iron fist, had a brutal reputation and had a dislike for the Welsh, so a worthy candidate for being a villain in future stories. He also went on the fifth, and failed, Crusade in 1218. Ranulf was one of the very few magnates to witness the signing of the Magna Carta of 1215, which he later adapted to appease his own Barons in the form of the Magna Carta of Chester. He later acted as an elder statesman in witnessing the re-issue of the Magna Carta in 1225. In reference to Robin Hood, the only episode that links Ranulf and Nottingham is that he had joined King Richard in March 1194 in an historic siege at Nottingham Castle, in order to put down the rebellion of King John.

This is interesting and ties in with Ranulf and King Richard, Nottingham and the crusades, but it lacks the relevance behind the stories behind Robin Hood himself. This may be where oral traditions crept in which influenced later stories, but I believe this to be a red herring in trying to establish the truth behind the real Robin Hood. So, who could this Randolph, Earl of Chester actually be? Well, there is one very fitting person that we know from history that fits in nicely with the stories, yet thanks again to the passage of time, the evidence is limited, and he wasn't in fact an Earl of Chester, yet he was still a very influential character in this same area at the time.

Ranulph de Mortimer

(Randolph, Ralf, Ralph, Raoul de Mortemer)

Ranulph was a marcher Lord of the Welsh Marchers (the border lands between England and Wales – Welsh 'Y Mers' and Medieval Latin 'Marchia Walliae'). This would include all counties that straddle the borderlands, but particularly related to Shropshire, Herefordshire and Cheshire. Ranulph was born in Normandy, date unknown, and died around 1104 (date again unknown). He was the son of the Norman Baron Roger de Mortemer. Ranulph gets his surname from the castle of Mortemer in Pays de Bray, Normandy, following his father taking the castle after the Battle of Mortemer against the forces of Odo (the brother of King Henry I of France). Ranulph's father had favour with Duke William following this episode, but then fell out of favour for harbouring an enemy (Count Ralph III, 'The Great', his father-in-law) and was subsequently banished together with losing all his lands in Normandy. He later gained pardon, but never regained the Castle Mortemer. It was down to his son, Randolph, who repossessed the property by grant of Duke William. So, Randolph de Mortimer basically means Ranulph of Mortimer, however Ranulph is the founder of the English House of Mortimer of Wigmore. He obtained Wigmore Castle after William Fitz Osbern's son, Roger de Breteuil joined the 'Revolt of the Earls' - 1075. These lands would have been granted to him by King William in line with his allegiance to the crown.

So, what has this Ranulph got to do with Robin Hood? Well, if we are to understand that there was a Ranulph associated with Robin Hood in the earliest reference to Robin Hood, then there must be some sort of a link there. The reference to Ranulph has been lost over time, but he would have been a Norman and as a result, the arch enemy of Robin. I would suggest then that this character was replaced by the more well-known Sherriff of Nottingham and also John Lackland (given he was also in line to the throne) and through the years, Ranulph was dropped due to the audience and focus of the time changing.

Regarding Ranulph, according to genealogy held at Wigmore Castle, Eadric held the castle against Ranulph in 1075 as he joined the Barons Revolt. This would have put Eadric on a collision path with Ranulph at this time – he would have been a fitting adversary. No doubt these two characters had dealings in the local area leading up to this episode and I think time will reveal more about the relationship these two had. There is another reference that it was Ranulph in relation to Eadric: 'after long struggles and handed over to the king for life imprisonment, some of his lands afterwards descending to the abbey of

Wigmore'. I cannot find where this reference originally came from, but it does state that after 'long struggles' meaning there was bad blood between these two people running up to the siege of Wigmore Castle. This adds extra value as to how subsequent stories developed and how they became the main opposing characters behind the ballads.

So, we have Eadric fighting against a Norman Lord and having 'long struggles' with him. Now there is a recipe for a story! But does this link in with the greater picture of Robin Hood?

OK, let's think back to earlier stories that might have influenced the storyline between Robin and his adversaries and why Robin was associated with May Day celebrations.

Robin and the Wren. Now quietly say to yourself…. 'Ranulf' and 'Wren' over and over again…. Change the way you pronounce them…. Now to me, this sounded very similar, which then got me thinking. So, I did a bit of research and found this:

> "Wrenroc" is a corruption of the Welsh name "Wrenoc" or "Wrenoch" which is sometimes interchangeable with Gronwy and Ranulph.

This was referenced as coming from Ancestry.com. I don't know how far this could be pushed, but 'Wren' could be the Welsh short name for 'Ralf' etc. Given that this is a Welsh reference, and these stories originated from the Welsh borderlands, then it seems that we have a link here with what might have influenced the reasons why Robin is associated with May Day, and also how this also linked in with this particular Ranulf. I understand the Welsh name for Wren is Dryw, but old English name was wrenne and even earlier references being wrænna. So, the name itself hasn't changed that much through the ages, but we now have a possible take upon Wren and Ranulf – hidden by the Welsh language.

Do we now have a human element to the fight between the Seasons. The Robin (Anglo-Saxon) representing warm, good and happier times and then the wren (Norman) representing cold, harsh and sad times. Is this how the people of the time tried to link the story behind Eadric and Ranulf? The Vikings would have been accustomed to this Pagan belief, so the Normans would have embraced this storyline during May celebrations. Plus, Robin (Robert) is a Norman name and not one associated with the Anglo-Saxons. One thing is clear, there was a long-held tradition behind a Robin being associated with the May and Summer celebrations, both Saxon and Norman.

It is also interesting to note that under Greek Mythology the Oak tree nymphs (fairies) were referred to as 'Dryads' which is too much of a coincidence that the Welsh name for Wren is 'Dryw'.

Above: Artistic image of the Wildman as seen in the famous Paterson Gimlin Film (1967).

Blown away? Now, if you are still reading this, then you are asking where this is all leading to... correct? I know it all sounds crazy so far, but I am not writing this book for fun, I have a viewpoint to tell here, and it carries some historical value. Well, I also knew that with the forest people there is always a double meaning behind what they tell you. This can sometimes be very confusing, yet they want you to work the rest out for yourselves. Many a night I have been awake trying to get my head around how everything links together and sometimes the pieces to this jigsaw puzzle fall into place. So, what has Enrith or Erith got to do with Robin Hood? Well, we have already seen how Robin is linked to the Green Man and the May Day festivities, Jack in the Green, the fairy folk etc. Well, how does this all come together then... and is it right that I get my leads from a forest person personally via telepathy? Can I be truly mad in putting this in print and staking my name and reputation on this? Well, just like in the Bigfoot community, people's attitudes change based upon new ways of thinking, experiences and collective discussions and critical thinking. So, right now, this book is way ahead of the curve in that capacity. Back to Enrith/Erith now. We have already established the name has a link to flowers – maybe even a link with the Roman goddess of the Wild – Flora. But that cannot be it, and it's not. We have already mentioned that Robin, the bird, was represented as the King of Summer, the Oak King, prior to the days of Robin Hood. And we know that Robin Hood is also the King of Summer at the May Day festivals. So, what is the Latin name for Robin, the bird (European variety)? Look it up before I tell you.... go on... I dare you…

Above: A picture of one of our local Robins.

Ok, if you had chance to look it up, then you will realise that the ancient Latin, and Greek, name is 'Erithacus' (which referred to a small bird but was commonly taken to relate to Robins). Erithacus, seriously? You can imagine my dismay when I found this out. Back in 2017 I was given the name Enrith/Erith... you can see this in one of the videos on Youtube where I mention this many years ago (How to make contact with the forest people - 18 May 2018). I was also told this years before I had even started researching for my first book – (which only started in the latter part of 2021, and regarding Robin Hood, I only started looking into this in the final months of 2023). This was too much of a coincidence, way too much! So how does this link in with Eadric? Well, given all of the stories told about Wild Eadric, he seems to have very strong links to the legend behind Robin Hood, could this then be correct? So, keen to research this further, it became apparent that an earlier Anglo-Saxon name and Latin name for Eadric is 'Eadricus'. So, we now have Eadricus and Erithacus. These two names are so similar sounding, just like Hood, Hode, Hoode... they have different spellings, yet they sound near the same or at least, very, very similar. These two names could easily become a corruption of each other when pronounced. But are they the one and same? Well, this is where we have to start looking at why the people of this time would have had Eadric celebrated in such a way. The people of this period were very unhappy and being treated unfairly and harshly. The Norman overloads were cruel. What they needed was 'hope', hope that the good times will return. And every year they would come together during May, or at the Summer Solstice and worship the Gods of Nature, the Green Man and request their help and they lived in 'hope' that they will be answered.

It is whilst writing this that it occurred to me that Robin would steal from the rich and give to the poor. We always understood that the statement meant that Robin gave the things that he stole from the rich and gave that to the poor, yet it does not exactly say that. Certainly, in later May Days, Robin would go requesting money from people and give the money collected to the poor, or to the Church. But maybe this statement was that Robin gave **'hope'** to the poor and not money. That would make much more sense in the context of the time and why he was celebrated as such at the May Day festivities.

Going back to Eadric or Eadricus, we can now see that a lot of the folklore stories make sense, some of the factual records about what happened to Eadric makes sense and now the name and reason also makes sense. But why do we not know the stories of Robin Hood as Eadric the Wild? Well, do you honestly think for a single moment that the Norman elite would allow Eadric, a man of resistance to their rule, would be allowed to become a major character celebrated every summer? He would become an icon of rebellion. So, some bright spark came up with an alias – Robin, which was more in keeping with a French name – Robert/ Robin and Hood, so at least the Normans would find the name Robin more acceptable, as it also related to the Viking God of Thor. Why Hood then? Well, at the beginning of the book I asked you to do an internet search for a 'hooded person' and don't you think that in itself was revealing? Can you see the face of the hooded person? Nearly all of the pictures you will see that the face is concealed, so, just like the name, this was all concealed (can you think of any other symbols from this time period that also has a face partially hidden by leaves?). Also, 'Hood' would stand as a personal attribute to the surname itself. It is also apparent that the Wildman was often called 'Hood' or 'Wood' in England. So yet again, a double strike of the meaning behind the name. Can this all be true? Does this finally answer the age-old question who was the person behind the legend. Did he really exist? Well, I had to ask my forest friend contacts if this was it… having finally joined up lots of the dots and yes, I got the answer that it was. Just like in my first book… I had linked Robin Goodfellow to Santa Claus, together with the Wild man. I confirmed that Shakespeare included Puck, a

Bigfoot, in his Midsummer Play. There was so much about our history that seems to be based upon fiction or oral stories, yet exaggerated, however, there is some truth that lies behind them. Fairies, goblins, elves and the likes, even Santa himself, are based upon stories that have had links to these magical forest beings.

Above: Medieval coin from 1577 representing the Wild Man, with an uprooted tree (confirming his strength) plus holding a candle (lights seen in the forest at nighttime – Willow the Wisp).

You might not appreciate this as being the case, yet you automatically follow traditions based upon previous held ideas – do you still leave out milk and cookies for Santa each Christmas Eve?

As I say, my first book records my 10 year journey leading me to understand how Santa is linked to the Wild man, he is indeed the Holly King of Winter. We now have the Oak King of Summer! We also now have an idea behind why there is an association between the May Day festivals and Robin Hood. He is the symbol of Anglo-Saxon propaganda of **'Hope'**! He is a symbol that survived those cruel days of a Norman takeover. Who are now to say that all of history is written by the victors! I can assure you that there are many more books and films written about the exploits of Robin Hood than there are about William the Conqueror. If we are to believe the stories from Shropshire about the ghost of Eadric, then he is still there in the background and in the faerie world protecting our lands at the time of adversity. Sometimes the truth is stranger than fiction… but I feel that Wild Eadric can now rest in peace, and we can celebrate the man behind the legend each, and every May Day.

Another coincidence

When thinking about Enrith and her links to Robin Hood, it became clear to me that with all of the Robin Hood tales, there is a link, not only to the Green Wood, and its magical qualities, fighting the Norman oppression, but also relying heavily on 'disguise' as part of a plot device. Was there anything else that I had overlooked? It was only recently that it dawned on me, yet was this just a coincidence or something that has been waiting 55 plus years to be told? We can now see that the truth about the real Robin was 'disguised' to conceal his true identity, he was a person of propaganda. In other words, it was a 'bluff' and the Normans swallowed it.. And where was the Patterson Gimlin film recorded? You guessed it – Bluff Creek! Can we now see that there was double meaning behind that famous encounter – the clearest recording of the Wild man ever recorded to date… and filmed at a place called Bluff Creek – or we can infer as a 'stream of deception'. And the name of the character being Erith, or Erithicus, meaning Robin?

Above: The local Robin that visits the Author's bird feeding table.

Definition of 'Bluff': an attempt to deceive someone into believing that one can or is going to do something. Or, to try to deceive someone as to one's abilities or intentions. This may also be linked to the 17th Century term of blindfolded or 'hoodwinked'.

I don't know, but certainly I gave up in believing coincidences when it came to dealing with the forest folk, yet I would like to think that this was the case. Either way, if we can now buy into the fact that the Normans were deceived, and we have been equally deceived for nearly a thousand years, then it all makes sense and yet it was a forest person who had opened the door to revealing the truth.

I am sure that a lot of you are thinking that this is too far-fetched. I understand this, and this is why I am more than happy to work with an academic institution to confirm that 1. the forest people are real, 2. the historical context adds up to what I am saying and 3. to confirm not just my account, but that of others who have joined me on this journey. Just like the current Bigfoot community, the landscape is changing, and we are not the only form of intelligent life on this planet, or indeed, the universe. Should we be scared? Having lived thousands of years alongside them, and in the past being called Robin Goodfellow and you inviting them inside the house on Christmas Eve each year? What do you think? They are good people... they are Good Fellows! But, and I stress.... don't end up on the naughty list!

Mora

Another coincidence?

Mora was the name of the ship that carried William the Conqueror to England. It was the fastest ship of William's 700 or more ships within his invasion fleet, and it arrived at the shores of England prior to the rest of his ships. It is bizarre that one of the four contacts I have with the forest people was Mora/Morah, which also had the Hebrew meaning of 'teacher'. Both Ricky and myself had seen her in a moonlit night time forest clearing in May 2019. Well, that turned out to be an understatement of the highest magnitude for me personally, like all the cryptic references I have for the other contacts. Again, just another pure coincidence that I am expected to believe! I can assure you that my journey into the Wildman of the UK has been a real education for me. It has been a real education for lots of other people too. Only now are we starting to turn the pages of our historical stories with a bit more relevance to a truer picture. Will people see some of Shakespeare's plays in a different light now?

One of the other contacts I had was Sol (Solomon) – and if you read my first book, then you will understand just how symbolic that was with my research into Santa and Robin Goodfellow. I have one more contact, my first, and I'm not too sure what that will relate to – but his name is 'Zach' (Zachariah).

Other food for thought

Homo sapiens, from the Latin, "Wise Man."

We know what the ancient Latin name for the Robin is, but what is the name for the Wren?

Well, the name used for it is more recent and only gained its scientific name in 1832 (Swainson), but it is called Troglodytes troglodytes (European variety). However, it is noteworthy that in 1758, in his edition of Systema Naturae, Linnaeus proposed a new species of human, Homo troglodytes given some references to primitive people and some that had coverings of hair or animalistic features. The word troglodytes referring to primitive characteristics – such as a cave man. Why did the wren get this name like this? Are we to understand that this purely refers to Wrens living in caves? Or does this link in with more historical links that the wren has with the wild man? It's certainly food for thought, and I have no way of confirming this either way.

Abbots Bromley Horn Dance

We are now off to Staffordshire to Abbots Bromley. Here we find a strange and yet ancient tradition that can at least be dated back to 1686 when the custom was first documented by Robert Plot in his 'Natural History of Staffordshire'. The 'horn dance', or more fitting description would be the 'antler dance' is a celebration using 10 main characters, 6 carrying mounted antlers (3 white and the brown coloured antlers, although the brown ones were painted blue in the past), a man on a hobby horse (Note: The use of the hobby horse was previously mentioned in 1532 and related to an ancient tradition, but did not mention anything about the antlers (Heaney 1987)). A jester, Maid Marian (who would be a man dressed up as a woman, which was normal during plays in the Middle Ages) and a young archer, who has been associated with Robin Hood.

The custom was understood to be an ancient tradition, and some believe that this can be traced back to performances as mentioned from St Bartholomew's Day Fair in 1226, unfortunately there is no concrete evidence to confirm this.

However, as one of the deer antlers broke in 1976, fragments were used for radiocarbon testing which gave a result of 1065 (+/- 80 years), so this helps indicate that the antlers are over 900 years old and must have been used many times before. The antlers actually come from a reindeer, which at the time were not native to the UK, so they are believed to have originated from Scandinavia, which would have been understandable given the Viking influences on the country around this time. So, I think we can be certain that the antlers held some important ritual purpose and like many other traditions, the symbolism has survived yet the true meaning behind this has been lost over the centuries.

During the time of Robert Plot, the antics would be performed at New Year and on 12th night. Through the ages this was also done during the Christmas period, and many believe this relates to the Winter Solstice. Currently it is held on the first Monday after the first Sunday following September the 4th.

What was its purpose? Well, just like the Cerne Giant, nobody knows, it's a mystery. Some suggest that it relates to hunting rites granted to the people of the village, others believe it relates to a dance prior to hunting (like we see North American native tribes doing prior to or following successful buffalo hunts). Others link it to the Winter Solstice. So, it's all a bit of a guess. Or is it? I have yet to see any reference to what I am going to suggest now.

OK, so let's break it down a bit. We know it's an ancient tradition, with the antlers dating back to Saxon times. We know from Star Carr that our Mesolithic ancestors did something very similar using the red deer antlers in their own rituals. We know that Maid Marion (which would have been a later added addition) was included in the performance. We know that an archer, associated with Robin Hood, was included. We know that a jester is also included. A jester? A court jester? Why would this be? Well, through previous research, it became apparent that the jester is a medieval take on the Green Man, like Robin Goodfellow. He was the lord of misrule and mischief. This is covered well by Phyllis Siefker in her book 'Santa Claus, Last of the Wild Men'.

So, going back to earlier pages, we know that the Pagan Forest God was Cernunnos. Part deer, part man – just like our Abbots Bromley dancers are meant to be. The dancers travel around the local area, covering around 10 miles at a time. This would indicate a ceremony tracing certain local boundaries, like staking territory. The huge antlers represent 'stags', long held understandings that they were the kings of the forest and highly respected creatures. The long-held beliefs passed down from earlier generations carried many superstitions. The fact that these dancers were associated with Robin Hood and the jester speaks volumes. Robin Hood was a figure related to fertility, the stags also carrying important symbolism associated with fertility. The season that these customs take place range from September through to around the solstice.... the deer rut season starts from as early as September through to the end of November/beginning of December; however a mild November/early December could see the rut approaching the time of the Solstice. This would not have gone unnoticed by our ancestors, and they would have witnessed these fighting bucks over the female herd. The winner takes it all. People would have heard the bellows echoing around the forests and knew what this meant – the approach of the solstice, when the battle between night and day would be decided. The mighty stags with all their power and might will fight each other for dominance within the forest and just like the new year, with new beginnings, they will lose their antlers and start to grow a fresh, bigger set in the new year. Cernunnos, just like the Green Man and Robin Hood represents new beginnings, fresh growth and with Robin Hood – it represents the fight against adversity. Yes, I believe the symbolism played out in Abbots Bromley performances is a mirror image to the long-lost rituals of our ancestors from 11,000 years ago, but modified over time to include characters from the middle ages and for good reason too.

Sutton Benger Church, Wiltshire

Sutton Benger has a quaint village church, All Saints Church, that dates back to the 12th Century together with a 15th Century tower added. Luckily, this place is only about 20 miles from me, and it exhibits one of the best Green Man sculptures in the country, as seen in one of the following pages. It is not possible to identify just how old it is, but it is believed that is has been re-touched in more modern times. As can be seen, the close connection the hidden man has with nature is clear to be seen, with birds pecking at what appears to be rose hips, so an autumnal representation I would say.

That said, the most revealing aspect to the Green Man can be found outside on the building corner lintels. On each of the corners of the building (apart from the corner where the later tower was added), you can see a Green Man sculpture, or what we can interpret as a Green Man. On one corner there is an Oak Summer Green Man (as seen below), and then there on another corner is another green man with more withered leaves (possibly winter?). The remaining Green Man is going to shock you. Remember these sculptures are very, very old – dating back over 500 years... but you can clearly see that the last sculpture is of an ??! (Go see....)

Above: One corner of the church and below a close up of the face.

Above: The shape of the leaves sprouting from the face appears to look like ivy, so this may be a representation of winter.

Above: On the opposite side to the possible winter king is the face with lots of acorns.

Above: A picture on the opposite side/corner – this possibly suggesting that this is the Summer King.

And what do we have represented on one of the other corners to the Church? Given that the 15th Century tower was built over the last corner, we have no idea what the fourth carving could have been, however I have my ideas about this, which I will share in a moment. But after all we have been talking about, you need to consider this……..

Above: the third corner of the Church and it's carving.

Above: And a close-up. I trust that you are seeing the same as me here, as recorded on a 12th Century Church. This is in association with the previous two carvings representing the seasons.

A representation of an ape on an ancient church building? Should that really be there? Well, I think after reading this book, you can start to see that there is a very genuine link there that has been staring us in the face for generations. Yes, this surely would be confirmation of the Green Man being associated with the Wild Man.

I am guessing that you are slightly shocked and maybe you even found this to be mind blowing. The fact of the matter is that these were represented back in the 1100's, and this was their way of dealing with this tricky subject that they had no understanding of. The Green Man was linked to the seasons but was also linked to the Wildman. The Wildman was not something of myth, they were recording things based upon what people had seen and trying to link this in with known creatures, in this case, some kind of ape. My previous book looks at this deeper, as Robin Goodfellow is linked yet again. Now the mystery behind the Green

Man, Jack in the Green, Willow the Wisp, Santa, Robin Hood, Fairies, Christmas traditions, how old beliefs evolved, plus lots, lots more…. can be looked at in a very different way.

Is Sutton Benger the only Church with these sorts of carvings? This is clearly a no, but I think this Church in particular is very good at putting it all into context. Now for my thoughts of what happened to the remaining carvings from the fourth corner. I am not sure if this is the case, but inside the church is recorded the best carving of the Green Man, and probably the best in the country. It is a superb carving, but it is believed to have been retouched in its history, so maybe not identical to the one from the 12th. Century, but it may give us an idea about its relevance to the others. And here it is..

Above: Amazing sculpture of the Green Man inside the church.

Above: Look at the detail here. The foliage sprouting out of the mouth of the Green Man. This confirms the ideas of how connected the green man was to nature, and therefore the seasons. It also confirms how concealed in nature the Green Man is – he is near **invisible** behind a covering of greenery.

Back to Robin Hood, after all, this is the reason for this book. Looking back at the May Day celebrations involving Robin Hood, it should be noted that at some point of the day, Robin dies or is killed and then shortly afterwards he arises, releasing the spirit of summer. The fact he is reborn is very revealing to the context that we have been talking about with the Wren and the Robin. So, let's take a look at the Holly King, which I touched upon in my previous book.

When you also look at the traditions involving 'Jack in the Green' – you will see a similar event happen. Jack will parade around the village followed by a host of people then he will dance and then he will die – allowing the death of winter and allowing the summer to begin. People can then take some of the foliage from Jack for good luck for the year. You will remember the story that I quoted linking Jack and Robin and the similarities are there – they both represent the 'Green Man'.

Now, can you think of any other festivals during springtime that involves someone dying and then being reborn? But I don't want to go there…

Here you can see some pictures from the Jack in the Green May Day celebrations from the neighbouring village to me – Highworth, in Wiltshire from May 2024.

Above: Jack in the Green May Day celebrations at Highworth.

We are seeing a revival in the Jack in the Green Celebrations around the country. In 2022, the Shakespeare Morris Dancers paraded the streets of Stratford Upon Avon for May Day with their Green Man which marked the revival of a tradition last seen in the Town in the 1870s.

It is also interesting to note that one of the biggest Jack in the Green Summer celebrations from around the whole of the country takes place at Hastings. Just imagine how ironic that is!

The Holly King

Above: Charles Dickens Christmas Carol –
The Ghost of Christmas Present – 1843.

If you are familiar with the story 'A Christmas Carol' by Charles Dickens, then you will understand that the second spirit was a green giant, who we accept as a representation of Father Christmas/Santa Claus. Above is an image of him from a Victorian story book. Note the holly crown around his head and that he is holding a fiery torch (or whisp). He is also dressed in green. Below I will quote a section from the Victorian version of a Christmas Carol, which you will see also links in with the death and re-birth of Robin Hood.

'It was strange, too, that while Scrooge remained unaltered in his outward form, the Ghost grew older, clearly older. Scrooge had observed this change, but never spoke of it, until they left a children's Twelfth Night party, when, looking at the Spirit as they stood together in an open place, he noticed that its hair was gray.

'Are spirits' lives so short?' asked Scrooge.

'My life upon this globe is very brief,' replied the Ghost. 'It ends to-night.'

'To-night!' cried Scrooge.

'To-night at midnight. Hark! The time is drawing near'

It is also worth noting that under the Ghosts robe, there were two hideous and miserable looking children – a boy and a girl.

'Spirit! Are they yours?' Scrooge could say no more.

'They are Man's,' said the Spirit, looking down upon them. 'And they cling to me, appealing from the fathers. This boy is Ignorance. This girl is Want. Beware them both, and all of their degree, but most of all beware this boy, for on his brow I see that written which is Doom, unless the writing can be erased. Deny it!' cried the Spirit, stretching out its hand towards the city. 'Slander those who tell it ye! Admit it for your factious purposes, and make it worse! And bide the end!'

...

The bell struck twelve.

Scrooge looked about him for the Ghost, and saw it not.

Above: Scrooge and the rapidly aging Ghost of Christmas Present.

Some valuable lessons can be learnt from this, but the focus is that this green giant, the second ghost, the Spirit of Christmas, is that he dies on Christmas Eve.... Allowing the spirit of summer to be released and to grow for the following six months and then the power of the Holly King overpowers the Oak King following the Summer solstice. We know that Robin Hood represents the Oak King and this explains why he must also die and be reborn at the May festivals. Just like Jack in the Green – when Robin is reborn then he releases summer! It's a repeated cycle.

Now... take a look at this medieval coin from Germany dating back to 1595 – here you can clearly see the wild man holding a fiery torch together with a holly crown. Is that just a coincidence? Obviously not, because when you start reading the historical references to Robin Goodfellow, then you will see there is a DIRECT LINK. And that links in with our modern representations of Santa Claus. My previous book confirms the things that you need to understand, yet I had no idea how this would then follow through to link in with Robin Hood.

Above: Medieval coin from Germany representing the Wildman. Notice any similarities with the Ghost of Christmas Present?

Notice the similarities? Here are a few hints.

- Wearing a Holly Crown
- Wielding a fire torch (or 'wisp') in his right hand.
- Bushy beard.
- Both linked to the Green Man
- There are some better coins available, but in the below image of one of my own coins, you can see the Wildman standing amongst triangular shaped trees.

Above: Picture of the Wildman, holding and standing within a load of 'Christmas Trees'.

So, have you ever wondered why you have a Christmas Tree in the house? And place a fairy upon it? And fairy lights? Take a look at this old coin and see what is represented in the background. Although you might think that the tradition of a Christmas tree dates back to Victorian times, and having been introduced by Prince Albert from a German tradition, but in fact the idea of bringing greenery (holly, ivy, ever green branches) into the house at this time of year for good luck was already a tradition during Pagan times. When you start looking at history you can trace some of the reasons why this was. Holly and ivy produce berries at this cold time of the year – which is at total odds to other plants, so they possessed magical properties. Indeed, mistletoe, with its white berries, is traditional for lovers to kiss underneath and if you wondered why this was, then you just need to crush a berry to understand why it is associated with fertility.

Above: Toby, the author's Labrador sitting next to the Christmas Tree, December 2022.

Note: Pagan beliefs are that the different Kings, who are indeed brothers, are reborn on their relevant equinoxes. The Holly King is defeated by the Oak King at Yule and the Holly King is then reborn on Ostara (spring equinox) in readiness to take the crown back from his brother at the summer solstice, when the Oak King's power and the sun and daylight hours peak. Given the defeat of the Oak King, there will be a gradual change as the leaves start to die off leading into autumn. The Oak King is then reborn at Mabon (autumn equinox) and when the sun weakens at the winter solstice, the Oak King strikes again leading to new growth in the spring. There are some variations to these beliefs, but in essence one brother is overthrown/dies and the other one thrives/reborn linked to the seasons. Can you think of anyone else that dies and is reborn around the time of the Spring Equinox?

Above: Red holly berries seen during the winter months and why the Holly King of winter gets his name from.

Above: Ivy berries seen during winter (together with a few red rose hips).

One last thing to add, and that is the inscription on (supposedly) Robin Hood's grave at Kirklees Park Estate, West Yorkshire. This is where Robin is said to have died, according to the early ballads. Is this based upon previous much earlier references, or is it just made up? Or does it hide the true origins behind the legend itself? Two versions of the epitaph for you to see – the original (Old English) and then the modern English translation:

> *Hear Underneath dis laitl stean*
> *Laz robert earl of Huntingtun*
> *Ne'er arcir ver az hie sa geud*
> *An pipl Kauld im robin heud*
> *Sick utlawz az hi an iz men*
> *Vil england nivr si agen*
> *Obiit 24 Kal Dekembris 1247*

And translated into modern English:

> *Here underneath this little stone*
> *Lies Robert, Earl of Huntingdon*
> *Never archer were as he so good*
> *And people called him Robin Hood*
> *Such outlaws as he and his men*
> *Will England never see again*
> *Obit: 24 December 1247AD*

So, Robin was meant to have died on December 24th, Christmas Eve, just like the Ghost of Christmas Present. Is that just another coincidence? Or is that confirmation to what we have already been discussing so far. My first book looked at the significance of Robin Goodfellow being associated with Christmas and how this all linked in with the pre-Christian (pagan) Roman festival of Sol Invictus. This was celebrated on the 25th of December as the birth of the 'Sun God' following the winter solstice. Christianity celebrates this date as the birth of the 'son of God'. As you can tell, there is an obvious overlap there, and now we have the death (and therefore re-birth) of Robin Hood at this same time. This is related to the symbolism that Robin has with the defeating the Holly King, and then the re-birth would be the period of growth, fertility and hope of the coming year.

In conclusion

I can appreciate that the content of the last part of this book is extreme, controversial and mind blowing. I get that. I have had over 10 years of experience dealing closely with the wild man of the UK, and I still find it hard to accept the ramifications of this myself. But I can assure you that they are real, very real. The people of this country understood this in the past, and this is where we get our associations with the Wildman/Green Man. Shakespeare and Charles Dickens are two people from bygone years that have made reference to these magical forest beings. So, I am now going to summarise what we have established and how this is linked in with the legend of Robin Hood.

- To our superstitious ancestors, the magical abilities of the wild man would have been explosive. They would understand that there were invisible forces surrounding them that are capable of extreme things. These would have sown the seeds to the birth of some of the Pagan religions and the need to worship Gods of the natural world. Star Carr may have given us an insight into this activity and how it first started.

- Over time, different cultures developed different beliefs about the magical forces around them. The Celts and the Norse cultures made the Robin and the Wren as symbols of the seasons. One as celebrations, and initially one as dread. The Romans and Greeks had their own Gods that related to different aspects of their lives, as well as the seasons.

- The summer and winter solstices were an important time in the prehistoric and medieval calendar. May Day, celebrated as the start of summer, was particularly important with no other month being valued as much. It was a time of happiness, merrymaking and a time of 'hope' for the future.

- May Day gods were associated with fertility, yet some also had close associations with Gods of war e.g. Inanna and of course, Mars Silvanus.

- Eadric was one of the first, if not the first, instigator of resistance to Norman rule after the Battle of Hastings. He joined forces with the Welsh to fight back and rather than facing the full force of a Norman army in open conflict, he used guerrilla tactics in attacking his foe. Hiding in the forests and hills of the Welsh borderlands, becoming **invisible** to his enemy. When opportunity allowed, he hit bigger targets such as Hereford and Shrewsbury.

- Eadric was labelled Silvaticus by the Normans (which was also a name used for the sprits of the woods), he was also called 'Eadric the Wild' – which links in with the Wild man. The English referred him and his band of men as 'Green Men'.

- There are many overlaps between the legend of Robin Hood and that of Eadric. There are folklore stories about Eadric being linked to the fairy world, which would also tie in with the wild man and would also tie in with the May Day celebrations.

- There is a 300 year period between Eadric's actions and the first reference to Robin Hood, so plenty of time for oral traditions to be altered in order to accommodate a more modern audience and why there are some possibles that only partly fit in with the storyline.

- To the Anglo-Saxons of the time, they would have wanted to conceal the identity behind the real person which led to the development of the character Robin Hood – he basically developed as an alias – but played the role of the robin (hope) duelling with the wren (dread) as a means of concealing the reason behind his character. The Normans would not have twigged, given the significance of the Robin to Norse beliefs. We can now understand how that alias developed and why Robin was a master of disguise.

- The influences of past legends have all morphed into the storyline of both Eadric and Robin Hood. Certain characters stick out, Eros the (invisible) archer, marrying a mortal, Psyche, and her quests. The Silvatici – and the guerrilla warfare techniques deployed by Eadric and Robin Hood and the (invisible) Robin Goodfellow and his link with the fairy world. Guerrilla warfare means that you become **invisible** to the enemy and strike when least expected. The Green Men of the forest are **invisible** to all, yet they are there (as you will see, these are depicted by the face hidden behind the foliage in stone/wooden carvings).

- Robin Hood represented the Summer Oak King at the May Day festivals. His adversary would be the Winter Holly King – the wren. Wrenoch is a Welsh corruption of Ranulf. The antics of Ranulf de Mortimer (a Norman Lord) and Eadric (an outlaw having had his lands disposed by the Normans) at a time of resistance, would have been the basis for many inspiring stories to the Anglo-Saxon community.

- Just like the alias of Robin Hood, there would be an alias behind Ranulf, Earl of Chester as stating Ranulf de Mortimer would clearly have been too much of a giveaway. Yet the area links in with Eadric, given this was the Welsh borderlands – and not Nottingham or Yorkshire.

- Rather than revealing the true identity of Eadric as a means of formal resistance, an alias was born. A true hero of the Anglo-Saxon people. One of a hooded man (hiding his identity) and this played in to the seasonal practices between the war between summer (good times) and winter (harsh times).

- If we consider the link that Eros has with the fairy world or land of the Gods, then Psyche, a human, becomes immortal after taking ambrosia.

- Folklore stories state that Eadric will return to protect England from foreign foes, and he can only rest once the lands have been returned to their former peacetime days. This confirms his duty to the Anglo-Saxon people. He represents the sole surviving resistance to the Norman takeover and his memory is still very much alive with us to this day.

- Eadric gave to the poor a sense of **'hope'** at a time of adversity, and this is a driving force behind the intentions of the May Day celebrations.

- Was it a coincidence that the Uprising of 1450 (part of Cade's Rebellion) that Thomas Cheyny took part – nicknamed Bluebeard the Hermit, leading a force from Eastern Kent, together with his rebel captains nicknamed 'Robin Hood', 'King of the Faries' and 'Queen of the Faries'.

- It is no coincidence that we see the development of the Green Man sculptures being used within churches from the early 12th century onwards. This carried a double meaning behind them. The green man represented the spirit of the woods (and fertility) and secretly, representing the green men symbolising resistance to Norman rule (the war elements being linked to the same Gods – Mars Silvanus).

- The name Eadric Child being associated with Lockley Woods, is that just a coincidence?

- Robin Hood's date of death being Christmas Eve. Again, is that just a coincidence?

- And as for the Wild Man of Bluff Creek, Enrith, and the hidden meanings behind that …. that is on a different scale entirely, yet for me, this is the confirmation that I was seeking!

If you feel that these findings are challenging, then you need to take a look at my first book in order to follow in my footsteps over the last 10 years, and then, I suspect, having your mind blown away again by the outcome of who was behind the real Santa Claus stories… But what I can say here, and am pleased to reveal, is that the magic associated with Santa is still very much alive to this very day! Santa lives! Yes, quite a bold statement. So, if you want to learn more, and why you leave out milk and cookies on Christmas Eve, then you need to keep that mind open and track down a copy of the book. Everything I have researched is based upon historical records, be it folklore or fact, the rest comes from thinking outside of the conventional box, experiences and linking up all of these apparent 'coincidences'. Do they add up or not? You are the judge, it is up to you to decide, but before deciding you need to appreciate that everything that we have been previously programmed to believe is not really the whole picture. So, good luck on your own journey of discovery… seek the truth and always keep an open mind.

Wild Eadric lives on!

- **Wild Eadric:** In 2005, the rose hybridists David Austin created the variety of pink English rose who he named in honour of Wild Eadric. It has a strong fragrance with hints of cloves, watercress and cucumber. How fitting is that, now considering the possible link Eadric has with the Roman Goddess 'Flora'.

- **Wild Eadrics Way:** This is a long distance footpath that is contained within the county of Shropshire. The path runs for 49 miles (79 KM) – following certain parts of the Shropshire way. The route follows from Church Stretton climbing up the Long Mynd and famous Striperstones and then falling downhill to Bishop's Castle. It uses a medieval drovers road together with the Portway and Offa's Dyke path to meet Clun and the Norman Clun Castle. It then travels towards an Iron Age hillfort at Bury Ditches and then on to Craven Arms and ending at Ludlow – which is the centre of the Welsh Marches.

  I hope to walk this path in the next few years, and I also hope that the legend of Robin Hood and that of Eadric can one day be recognised as the same.

- Eadric will ride again. This time, I understand that the enemy is closer to home.

Final thoughts to ponder on

I just want to take a moment to contemplate upon the implications this all has. Are we to accept that the name Enrith/Erith was given to me back in 2017 was pure coincidental? Think about that for a while.

The names of the other contacts that I was given included 'Sol' (meaning the sun), which also had a massive influence upon my previous book where the Roman Festival of 'Sol Invictus' played a major role in the findings, but also links in with this book too. And now we know that the Normans were deceived into accepting 'Robin', including Robin Hood within the May Day festivals – yet with a hidden meaning behind its relevance. That tradition has survived and only grown in significance since those very dark days that fell upon England. So indeed, it was a 'bluff' and it worked.

So, having Erith/Enrith turning up in the way that she did at 'Bluff Creek', are we to accept that this was pure coincidence yet again? Or has all of this been staged leading up to this revelation? If so, then isn't this the most remarkable story of the 21st Century?

I would also like to add that within the Christian faith, we understand that the Devil is a fallen angel from Heaven. We now understand that Pan, Robin Good Fellow etc. are all referred to as the Devil. Please also note that Santa is an anagram of the word Satan, that is no coincidence. This would also suggest that these forest folk are linked to angels in some way, as far as religion is concerned. Now why would the Church want to create real life Pagan symbols of nature as evil and get people to follow their own take on God? Why would the Church also want Santa to be linked to a 4th century Saint? Well, that is too deep a subject for me for today… but one for the reader to ponder upon.

Finally, I just want to say that this book has given me many hours of confusion, headaches and restless sleep as I tried to join all the dots to understand how this all fitted together. For the reader, I don't know what you are personally thinking right now, but I am sure that you are deep in thought too or saying this is just too much. I understand this and I guess only time will tell if these findings are accepted, but I do want to confirm, with hand on heart, that the Wildman of the UK is real, very real. It would be easier to understand the findings of this book by accepting this challenging idea. So, I am here offering an open invitation for an academic institution to work with me in gaining the acceptance to the things I have said. I will add that on my quest, a number of years ago, I approached Professor Bryan Sykes of Oxford University to come just 30 miles down the road to take a look for himself with what I was faced with. Considering he had been thousands of miles around the world undertaking a DNA study into the existence of the Wildman, then 30 miles and an afternoon would not be too much to ask. Alas, it was. All he wanted was definite proof before leaving his office. Well, our paths did not cross following this, but it did make me chuckle when I saw Wildman activity in a forest located just outside Oxford. Unfortunately, Professor Sykes has now passed away, otherwise he might have changed his mind about that 30 mile road trip. So, the offer is there for another institution to get involved, but I won't be holding my breath in anticipation.

Regarding the historical context I have quoted in this book, all I can say is that I have done my best to reference the facts as I researched them. Some of these may be open to interpretation, and if I have quoted anything incorrectly, or excluded clarity, then this is an omission on my behalf, but I am certain these points will be minor or mis-quoted which I have followed elsewhere etc. So, I thank you for reaching this part of the book and for taking this journey of discovery with me. The world truly is a magical place now!

Finally, one last thought...

Is it just a coincidence that the sole surviving person to witness Enrith/Erith at Bluff Creek in 1967 is called 'Bob' (Bob Gimlin). Bob being related to 'Hob' (hobgoblin – i.e. the wildman) and is also a popular and short name for Robert – which Robin is also derived from. Could this be yet another double meaning behind that encounter, or just another coincidence, like all the others we are led to believe?

It does make you think, doesn't it!

Have we finally identified the man behind the Myth?
The true hero behind the Anglo Saxon Legend from England?

Above: Robin Hood's last shot arrow.

Testimonial by Ricky Bailey

Above: Ricky standing next to one of the standing stones along the Avenue at Avebury Henge.

If you have already obtained a copy of Paul's previous book 'Bigfoot it's a Fairy Tale', you will be aware now that I have been a contributing partner on this journey for over a decade. Hours upon hours, Paul and I have together amassed research material related to the forest people here in the United Kingdom. Our persevering courage at the very beginning, soon swiftly began to be replaced with curiosities, questions and eventually some answers to the things we were witnessing as the years went on. Today, the rise in our understanding has, as of now, brought us closer to the forest people than we could have both ever imagined.

This latest edition of our journey truly hits home, merging the tales of folklore between two iconic symbols of the woods together in a way that has never before been examined and as such explored in any great depth. The existence of the UK's own hooded figure has been debated for centuries. Some believing Robin

Hood being based on a real person, while others see him more in a fictional sense, simply as a symbol of hope against tyranny. A warm summer's day perhaps after a cold winter's night. Regardless, the folklore and ballads surrounding him have shaped cultural narratives on justice and heroism that have inspired a nation. Yet despite this, we really have no concrete name and, as such, a resting place for this hooded figure of ours, revealing perhaps many intriguing parallels that this book hopes to examine between Robin and the forest people. And by aligning them, this book hopes to reveal the long-lost connections between these two legendary icons, examining in detail their shared origin and thus broadening the implications the forest people now hold on our own, British history. This is our story, our annual dance between the Robin and the Wren.

We have come a long way to get to the stage we are at now. Paul's solid commitment to this project over the many years is truly commendable. The combination of field experiments and background research myself and a select few others have witnessed, has allowed Paul to, as it were, reverse engineer our forest friend's history through the ages. This has resulted in the forecast of many coincidences and similarities, discovered quite often before they have even been hypothesised. And it is that reason alone as to why I fully endorse this book in its entirety and hope that you, the reader, once again relish the information it contains.

Above: The author and Ricky in one of the rare pictures of us in the night-time forest.

Testimonial of Gem Glover

I have been married to Paul for over 10 years now and during this time I have heard many accounts of Paul and Ricky's adventures whilst in the forest, dealing with the forest people. I generally keep out of this as this is Paul's interest and my own interest is limited and for good reason, as it scares me sometimes thinking about it. But on numerous occasions I have ventured out to the forest with Paul, Ricky and others, during the day and at nighttime, and I have seen things that science has not yet explained. I was present on a video from the 21st April, 2016 on the Anglosasquatch Youtube channel. The video in question is 'British Bigfoot – our resident sceptics view on things' – where I also witnessed the lights (or we now know as orbs) that were being mentioned in the video. I was also present on the video from the 24th of June, 2017 where we heard daytime wood-knocks, which was quite unusual (Sasquatch daytime woodknock recorded 24th. June, 2017). These videos were from the early stages of Paul's research and since then I have seen so much more. This now includes many more orb like lights flashing around us, at a distance, and also close by, different smells, changes in energy, together with shadow figures standing right next to us, and next to the device that Paul uses to gain their attraction. How does this all fit together? I have no idea, but Paul has traced back in history how these forest beings show up and this includes references to Shakespeare, Charles Dickens, Robin Goodfellow and Santa, Willow the Wisp – and now Robin Hood. My mind is completely blown, but I strongly believe that Paul has hit upon something of significance that will require further research that will help confirm his theories. My journey with Paul has been an amazing one and I endorse his work. Over to you now Science and Academics to follow-up on this….

Above: Happy days researching in the forest with Paul.

Testimonial of Robert Toplis

The UK Wildman is real. Very real. They have powers that we cannot comprehend. The saying curiosity killed the cat is very appropriate with my report. Parts of this you will find unbelievable, yet it is certainly an experience that I never want to relive.

My story started a number of years ago, initially in December 2019. I had a passing interest in the subject of the Wildman in the UK and was interested in learning more. I was at the time located at Matlock, Derbyshire and there were numerous local forests that I use to go mountain biking in. Well, given all the national reports about the Wildman, I thought I would do my own investigations into this. I started to hide long recording microphones at locations near to myself, near a trainline, river and a canal and instantly, to my dismay, I started picking up weird sounds that I could not attribute to natural or native UK wildlife sounds. These recordings just inspired me even more to carry on with this research, so I actively pursued this with a massive determination, and this is where I started to cross the line into using more deceptive techniques. This included covering the infra-red beam on trail cameras, going out late at night and chasing after sounds with my e-bike at speed. Cycling down pathways silently which I believe upset their normal nocturnal habits. Basically, doing everything intrusive in their locations, and showing no respect to their privacy. I ignored an invisible bluff charge, ignored two high/low frequency growls at me and continued to hide equipment around the local area where I knew there was activity. During my time, I was able to understand their chosen areas and I showed no fear in chasing after that illusive proof. I did see a tree peeking figure at one point along the canal path.

Then, the tides turned, and I was now the target, March 2020. I started hearing angry growls and noises, like banging outside of my apartment. My electronics within the apartment started playing up, strange interference, weird owl sounds outside the apartment (note: there was a cliff and trees directly outside my apartment where they targeted me from). I now knew that they were coming after me, yet I did not understand any of this. Within my apartment, late one night, I was laid out on my sofa, and I happened to gaze out of the window, and I saw two massive bigfoot like beings with glowing red eyes and swaying whilst watching me. I didn't know they could have glowing eyes, and I was just staring at them, but I didn't understand what I was looking at. The following night I was targeted in a huge way, I was bombarded with infra sound, and it was clear to me that they wanted me out. The feelings I had was fear, head fog, headaches, feelings of impending doom, I really felt that worried and I couldn't sleep. The attacks first started at nighttime, but then this developed to a lesser degree within the daytime.

I ended up getting more aggressive towards them as I was very angry too. At this point I did not appreciate the supernatural aspect related to them. I would go out a hurl abuse at them, and I ended up being attacked even further. I then tried the approach of apologising to them, but this didn't work either. I had opened Pandora's box and was now paying the price.

I had put up with this for three months, but then felt I had no choice but to move out. They had beaten me. This was starting to affect my mind and health. It was after 3 to 4 months that I was forced to move home and try to escape from this. I moved 12 miles away to Chesterfield, to a place with a roof apartment, thinking this was far enough away but unfortunately, they followed me there. I was now becoming a wreck, and I was alone dealing with this all the time. I was now starting to appreciate that they had supernatural abilities as I started hearing them walking on the roof. This hit me hard, so the more research I did into the subject of paranormal bigfoot, then I realised that they could be invisible to you, yet they were real. I started seeing glowing red orbs outside of the apartment windows and it just got crazier. The infra sound was a constant at nighttime and there was no escaping it. I tried to defend the one room in my apartment with sound proofing, loft insulation at the window, foil at the doors and air bed mattresses around the walls. Anything I could do to prevent or reduce the infra sound, including wearing ear defenders. I put up with this for a further four months and then I went to my brothers to stay with him.

Although they did harass me there occasionally, they would keep clear when I was with other people, so this was a welcome relief. I stayed with my brother for four months and during this time I was signed off work due to stress and anxiety.

I was starting to feel the pressure that other people would not believe me, including my family. They were possibly starting to think I had gone mad. I had been called a hoaxer by the online UK bigfoot community, so having thought about this, I wanted to prove to people I was telling the truth, so I spent £400 on a lie detector test (as attached), which I wanted to confirm that I was telling the truth. I didn't have to do this, but it was my own way of proving that I had been witnessing these things.

I didn't want to go back to the old place, so I moved to another place in Chesterfield, now knowing that these beings were supernatural. This was located above a shop. At the new place they left me alone for a while, but then they started coming back to me again. It was then around December, 2023 that I first made contact with Paul through a Facebook group. He worked with me in trying to resolve the issue with the forest folk. We tried a few different things and some of this made things worse and some slightly better, but at one point we made a breakthrough, and I am pleased to say that everything has changed. The bad energies have all gone and I actually feel much happier now than when I first started to look into this topic. So, my advice to other people is to show respect to forces that you do not understand. I regret my aggressive techniques in trying to obtain proof, it worked against me. My reaction to them, anger etc. was not very nice, which also did not help matters. I lost four years of my life in a bad way, but I can appreciate why this happened now as I didn't heed the warning signs. There is a reason why the people of old use to leave out bread and milk for the 'fairy folk' – they understood, and I can appreciate that now.

Examiner: C.M van den Berg
Mobile: +447570815628
Email: buks.vandenberg@liedetectortest.uk

CONFIDENTIAL POLYGRAPH REPORT

NO DECEPTION INDICATED   Private & Confidential

DATE OF EXAMINATION

Monday 28 September 2020

MAIN ISSUE

The following person asked to undergo a polygraph test to determine if he was telling the truth when he stated that he saw a Cryptid and that he was driven from his home by the Cryptids.

Robert Toplis

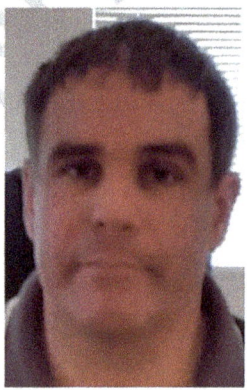

ROBIN HOOD: SILVATICI

The examinee supplied our examiner with the following personal details.

BOOKING REF:	:	646337CDBE
Name	:	Robert
Surname	;	Toplis
D.O.B.	:	24 March 1979
Age	:	41
Address	:	███████████████ Chesterfield
Education	:	NVQ Level 3
Occupation	:	Hetas Builder
Employed At	:	███████████
Employed Since	:	23 years
Marital Status	:	Single
Name of Partner	:	N/A
Occupation of Partner	:	N/A
Health	:	Good
Children	:	None
Previous Arrests	:	None
Criminal Record	:	None
Previous Polygraph Test	:	None

PRE-EXAMINATION PHASE

Before commencement of the polygraph examination, a statement of consent was signed stating that the examinee underwent the examination voluntarily.

During this interview, the Polygraph Examiner explained the polygraph instrument and the different sensors used for measurement to the examinee.

The case history was also discussed with the examinee, debriefing the examinee of any information regarding the issues and circumstances under investigation, and thoroughly reviewing the test questions and the examinee's intended answers for that particular phase.

The examinee stated the following:

- The examinee stated that he saw a cryptid.
- He stated that he saw some structures that he assumed were built by the Cryptids.
- He stated that the structures were made from branches and bent over trees.
- He stated that he took a waterproof phone and he managed to record some sounds on it over a period of a few months.
- He stated that he saw a cryptid on several occasions.
- He stated that he moved away from his previous residence as the Cryptids harassed him by emitting low frequency sounds outside his residence

Upon completion of the pre-test interview, the examiner determined the examinee to be suitable for the polygraph technique. Upon review of the polygraph test questions, the examinee indicated that he completely understood the scope and meaning of each question.

EXAMINATION

A Lafayette computerized polygraph system, model LX4000 was used for the collection of polygraph tests (test data). This instrument makes a continuous recording of autonomic responses associated with respiration, electrodermal activity, and cardiovascular functioning. The instrument also includes sensors designed to record peripheral behavior activity and cooperation during the examination. A functionality check prior to the examination confirmed the instrument was in proper working order.

LieDetectorTest.uk associates themselves with Polygraphist's who received Internationally Accredited Training accepted by the American Polygraph Association.

The services of an interpreter had not been requested by the examinee; the examination was conducted in English.

A MGQT Test was utilised by the Polygraph Examiner using a fully computerized multichannel polygraph instrument, that is capable of simultaneously recording both thoracic and abdominal respiratory and muscle/behavioural activity, along with changes in cardiovascular and electro dermal activity, and includes dedicated components to monitor test subject behaviour and assist in the accurate differentiation of test data that represents authentic sympathetic/autonomic response activity to test stimulus questions from data that includes adulterated autonomic and peripheral/behavioural nervous system activities intended to alter or defeat one's polygraph test results.

A series of three test charts were completed. Careful inspection of the examinee's polygraph examination record revealed test data of sufficient interpretable quality to complete a standard numerical evaluation in order to render a qualified opinion regarding these test results.

Questions put to the examinee amongst others:

- Did you see what you know for sure to be a Cryptid? (Yes)
- Was the sole reason for leaving Matlock because you were being harassed by the Cryptids? (Yes)
- Did you lie to anyone about your Bigfoot experience? (No)
- Did you lie when you said that you saw Cryptids more than 4 times? (No)

The examinee answered to the questions as indicated above.

CONCLUSION

The examinee's polygraph test did not contain any significant physiological responses on the relevant questions.

It is the opinion of our examiner that Robert Toplis was honest when he answered to the relevant questions on the test.

The examinee can be excluded from further investigations.

The question set was administered using a MGQT question test, as it is a recognised, reliable and validated test technique approved and validated by the American Polygraph Association and the British Polygraph Association.

POST-EXAMINATION PHASE

After the examination was concluded, the examinee signed a statement of release stating that he was treated in a fair and respectable manner and that he understood all the questions asked during the examination.

CM van den Berg
FORENSIC PSYCHO-PHYSIOLOGIST
MARYLAND INSTITUTE OF CRIMINAL JUSTICE (MICJ)
AMERICAN POLYGRAPH ASSOCIATION

EXAMINER-CREDENTIALS

The Polygraph Examination was conducted by **C. M van den Berg**. He successfully completed his training as a Polygraph Examiner at the **Maryland Institute of Criminal Justice**. He has been keeping abreast with the latest technology and advanced training in his field of expertise. C.M. van den Berg is an accredited member of the **American Polygraph Association.**

Above: (June 2023) Rob's attempts at reducing the effects of infrasound in his apartment.

Note from the author

Yes, it is hard to believe the above account, but this is a very extreme situation that Rob has been through, and luckily, he is out the other side now and learnt a very valuable lesson. How can we relate to this from history? Is there a naughty and nice list that people end up upon? Where did that idea come from and why did the people in the past leave out bread and milk in order to appease the fairies? My own accounts have been good ones and that is because I showed respect from the very start, so I must be on the nice list (hopefully). It goes without saying that sometimes you can upset them, and they let you know. Below is a picture of my car's battery being drained overnight whilst on an overnight stay at a research location of ours. The RAC man did not understand why the battery had failed as it was still showing as OK, yet there was absolutely no power in it. We dare not tell him what we thought had caused it… but he was confused with his test equipment. They do give you warnings if you have upset them, so you need to heed them, otherwise you can end up telling a story like Rob has. Yes, they have abilities, and these abilities would have been like pure magic to the people of a bygone age, indeed, as they are to us today!

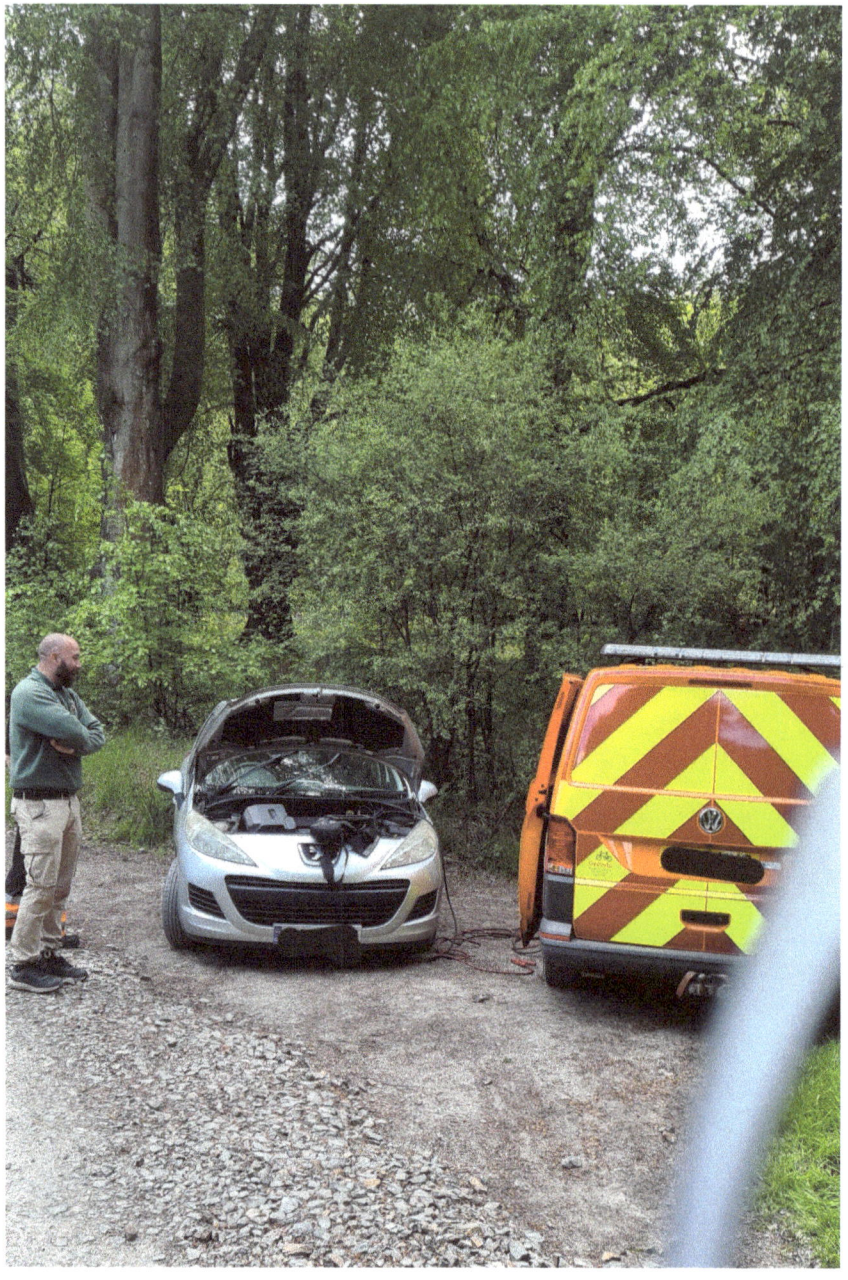

Above: Summer 2024. The car battery got drained overnight by factors we cannot understand.

Additional pictures to ponder upon

Above: The author with the Merry Crowd that follows Jack in the Green. May 2024.

Above: The Morris dancers using wooden sticks – possibly linked to the Wildman 'wood-knocks'.

Above: Jack in the Green – notice the 'crown' that he wears.

Modern Day research for the Green Man

Above: The author stood next to a 'ground stick' that has been stuck in the ground by the forest folk. This possibly indicates a territorial marker, but to this day, it remains unclear.

Above: The atmospheric 'Goldilocks' research area.

Above: Believed fingernail markings next to multiple sapling breaks.

Above: Star shaped 'glyphs' found in the forest – a type of forest language.

Above: Pinned tree arch. Natural or made by the Wildman? That is the challenge to understand.

Above: Ricky standing next to a fresh ground-stick at the research location.

Above: Green Man as represented in the woodwork at Gloucester Minster.

Above: Santa, from 1910, as depicted prior to the days that Coca-Cola got involved.

Above: A green Santa, a Robin and a sprig of Holly.

Above: Another green Santa from 1912.

Above: Artistic representation of Enrith/Erith by Arfon Jones

Above: There is Wildman standing just to the left of this tree, but he is **invisible** here. It is only when your eyesight adjusts that you can make out slight distortions to the energy/vibrations present.

Above: Artistic representation of a light anomaly the author saw on the 4th. of October, 2015 at the Goldilocks zone.

Above: Medieval hairy Wildman coin from Germany holding a candle in the dark – this was a clear link to Willow the Wisp lights as seen in the forests.

Above: Another two examples of the Wildman carrying candles in the forests.

Above: Possible fingerprint taken from a baiting station experiment, July 2015.

Above: Another example of a sapling break together with associated nail marking features.

Above: An X shape structure positioned very close to the nighttime research spot. These were stuck in the ground making the X shape. January 5th 2019.

Above: Believed Wildman caught on film, June 4th, 2015. This footage was also associated with a bright flash of light prior to it's emergence.

Above: Drawing of a nighttime encounter seen on thermal camera July 16th, 2015.

Above: 13th March, 2016. An interesting glyph like marker.

Above: The author next to a newly found ground stick – June 9th, 2015.

The Author

Given the extraordinary claims being made in this book, it is only fair that I give a little bit more background information regarding myself. I have a degree in Geological science from Plymouth and have a very active interest in history – be it pre-historic or related to more modern times. My interest into the Wildman took over 10 years ago, and this has absorbed a lot of my time and energy in researching into this. I had no idea where this would lead me to, but my two books are the culmination of this roller-coaster adventure of mine. In the below pictures you can see myself, together with a national treasure – Sir David Attenborough. I had created some fossil replicas for a few of his documentaries and had the good fortune and opportunity to meet him on one of the filmsets.

My last words are for the Forest People who I have over the years befriended. It has truly been a remarkable adventure and one that I will cherish for the rest of my Life. Thank you!

Above: A picture of the author together with Sir David Attenborough during filming in 2010.

Above: Sir David Attenborough looking at the author's replica fossil of 'Darwinopterus' whilst on the film set.

www.ingramcontent.com/pod-product-compliance
Lightning Source LLC
Chambersburg PA
CBHW042139160426
43201CB00021B/2338